CONTENTS

Hawaiian Islands

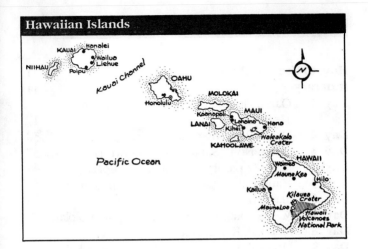

492 A.D.

A thousand years before Columbus's celebrated voyage, double-hulled canoes from Tahiti sailed to windward for thousands of miles, using ancient navigational techniques, to arrive at a legendary "heavenly homeland of the north." Near where these Polynesian mariners landed, a former sacrificial temple shares the lava and lush tropical landscape with opulent resorts and simple tents pitched on stunning white sand.

Welcome to Hawaii, where contrasting vacation pleasures, lavish and simple, manage to coexist with riddles rooted in both its Polynesian and volcanic origins. *2 to 22 Days in Hawaii* guides you, mile by marvelous mile, through 6 of the 132 islands, reefs, and shoals that make up the Hawaiian archipelago: Oahu, Maui, Molokai, Lanai, Hawaii, and Kauai.

Take your time. Travel from one end of the chain to the other, from the youngest island to the oldest, and be utterly surprised and startled by the differences, both obvious and subtle. Since you can fly between any two islands for about the same low price, arrange the sequence of islands in any way you wish.

2 to 22 Days in Hawaii starts on Oahu, where the windward and north coasts completely contrast with Honolulu. Oahu is rich in history and culture and as beautiful as the other islands (although more crowded). Don't bypass Oahu because you mistakenly equate the whole island with Waikiki's commercialization. From Waikiki, travel on to the windward coast and the Banzai Pipeline. Cameras will click above and below water. Proceed to Maui, the second-largest island and fastest-growing tourist destination. Visit Lahaina, the splendidly rejuvenated historic whaling town. Experience Haleakala vistas from the summit outlook and within the crater. Discover upcountry Maui on the volcano's slopes. Travel the amazing road to blissful Hana. Discover the remote beaches of western Maui, beyond the Kaanapali and Kalapapa resorts and the beaches of Makena beyond Wailea.

Old Hawaii can still be found on Molokai, especially
east Molokai, together with some of the most spectacular
island scenery at Kalaupapa Peninsula, the famous leper
colony beneath 2,000-foot cliffs; the twin waterfalls of
Halawa Valley; and hidden beaches around the western
coast.

On Lanai, a scenic, pine-covered mountain ridge opens
up breathtaking views of neighboring islands and then
leads to one of Hawaii's most beautiful beaches as well as
to bays adjoining historic sites. The island's huge pineapple
plantation has faded into history. Two new resorts, one on
the shore and one in the mountains, offer different vacation
experiences and outstanding shared recreational facilities.
Lanai also has some of Hawaii's most remote, undeveloped
beaches.

The Big Island, dominated by two 13,000-foot volcanoes, invites hiking and exploring on windward and leeward coasts, including the opposite towns of Hilo and
Kailua-Kona. After 10 years of volcanic activity, Kilauea
may still be spouting lava when you arrive. You can travel
from lush Waipio Valley on the wet Hamakua Coast to
adjoining Waimea grasslands or volcanic wastelands to bril-
liant orchid gardens, in a matter of minutes to a few hours.
The Big Island has a half dozen of Hawaii's most dazzling
beaches, white and black, it's largest and best preserved
historic sites, and North America's largest ranch and only
commercial coffee-growing farms.

End the journey on Kauai, with incredibly varied cli-
mates and terrain on one small island, some of the best
hidden beaches and hiking trails in the chain, and unforgettable mountain and valley jungle scenery. Calling spectacular Waimea Canyon the "Grand Canyon" on Hawaii is
no exaggeration. In combination with the adjoining Na Pali
mountains and coastline, Waimea Canyon becomes one of
the wonders of the world. Dozens of excellent hotels and
other accommodation choices are scattered between
Poipu's beaches and hotels and the Princeville Resort
paired with Hanalei.

The itinerary format in this book is divided into 22 daily
sections, each containing:

1. A **suggested schedule** for each day's travel and sight-seeing.

2. Detailed **transportation** and **driving** directions.

3. **Descriptive overviews** and **sightseeing highlights** (rated in order of importance: ▲▲▲ Don't miss; ▲▲ Try hard to see; and ▲ See if you get a chance).

4. **Restaurant, lodging**, and **nightlife** recommendations.

5. **Itinerary options**—excursion and adventure suggestions for travelers who have extra time.

6. User-friendly **maps** of each island, with more detailed maps of major areas on the tour.

All local telephone numbers omit an area code since all Hawaiian Islands share one area code: 808.

How Much Will It Cost?

The variety of inexpensive or moderately priced accommodations and eating places on every island make it easy to stay within budget in the Hawaiian Islands. Use this book to make your accommodations, dining, activity, and travel choices, and your entire trip, including airfare, can average less than $225 per day for one person for a 7-day trip. As of this writing, round-trip airfare to Hawaii from anywhere in the U.S. is still close to its lowest level in years. Consequently, for two people, the trip cost comes down to about $150 per person per day, including both airfares. For two persons, there is no extra cost for car rental and very little extra cost for accommodations. Of course, the total and per diem average will be much lower for campers, hikers, cyclers, and travelers determined to maintain a strict ultra-budget itinerary.

Climate

Hawaii has two seasons, winter and summer. The main differences are the amount of rain and much less so the temperatures, especially from place to place. The average temperature year-round is 75 degrees Fahrenheit. Between the warmest weather in August and the coldest weather in January, the daytime temperature may vary 5 to 7 degrees. February is the most unpredictable month.

Temperatures depend on elevation. In summer, get over the 2,000-foot-level and it's definitely cooler; temperature drops three degrees for every 1,000 feet of elevation. But it also rains more in the mountains, especially on the windward side.

The weather in the off-season travel period (April through December 15, and especially April to mid-July and September to Christmas) actually may be better than the weather during high season. However, it can rain hard and long in winter. Even on the dry Kohala coast on the Big Island, it can rain on and off for weeks in January. In the Hilo area, over 210 inches of rain fell in 1991. Usually it's possible to find at least partly clear skies somewhere on an island even when it's raining somewhere else. Frequently, you'll see rainbows along with rain or mist.

Each island has a wet (windward) and a dry (leeward) side of the mountains. Trade winds blow on the northeast sides of mountains almost every day in summer, keeping the heat and humidity down, and frequently disappear in winter when you don't need them to moderate the temperature. When hot Kona winds take over from October to April, the temperature is cooler on the leeward side. As a result, notwithstanding occasional hurricanes, horrendous downpours, and bad Kona storms, nowhere in the world is the temperature more constant, moderate, and comfortable all year round.

Getting There

Airline fares can be so confusing and changeable, from season to season and city to city, that the only sensible advice is to shop systematically through your travel agent or, better yet, through several travel agents to compare prices, since some agents tend to favor certain airlines. Prepare your detailed itinerary for arrivals and departures on the islands, rental cars, and either hotel or price preferences. Start by asking for the lowest airfare, without prepurchase requirements, *packaged with car rentals*, for the day of the week on which you prefer to leave the mainland.

If you plan to stay at first-class hotels on any or all of the islands for some or all of the nights, *look at what the packagers can offer, combining airfare, car rental, and hotels.* One of the wonderful aspects of the islands is that you can select a convenient base on any island, without driving excessively for sightseeing.

Interisland Travel

Interisland flights between the major islands (Oahu, Maui, Kauai, and the Big Island) are so frequent that you only have to wait a few minutes to catch the next one. Hawaiian Airlines will get you between all of the islands, including Lanai and Molokai, flying DC-9 jets and 50-passenger Dash-7 four-engine turboprops. On the mainland, call 800-367-5320 for reservations. Aloha flies Boeing 737s. On the mainland, call 800-367-5250.

The maximum cost of one-way flights between islands on both airlines has increased to $69.95. However, the cheaper fare on the first (5:30 a.m. or 6:30 a.m.) and last flights (6:50 p.m. or 7:55 p.m.) is $49.95.

The Maui-to-Molokai ferry service offered by Sea Link of Hawaii, Suite 230, 505 Front Street, Lahaina, HI 96761, 661-5318, on the *Maui Princess* has not attracted enough passengers to prove successful. See if the service is still operational. The $42 round-trip boat trip from Maui to Kaunakakai, Molokai, is well worth the price. The 118-foot, four-prop craft has an air-conditioned main cabin and an open deck above. You can leave Maui at 7:30 a.m. and arrive on Molokai at 8:45 a.m. The trip can be packaged with accommodations on Molokai. This is another way to get a look at humpback whales in the channel between the two islands.

Car Rentals

Only on Oahu can public transportation (TheBus) take you wherever you want to go in the 22-day itinerary (in fact, everywhere on the island) at the lowest fare in the hemisphere. On the Big Island, the MTA has cheap (but slow) bus service that won't take you to coastal Puna. MTA's Hele-On Bus will take you cross-island from Hilo

to Kailua-Kona, and daily buses run as far north as
Waimea but not to the tip of North Kohala at Hawi. On
Lanai, you need a four-wheel-drive vehicle to see the
Munro Trail and on some of the off-the-beaten track
roads to the north and east of Lanai City. You won't need
a four-wheel drive on any other island unless you're
determined to really get off the beaten track, in which
case you'll pay at least $85 per day.

For rental cars, the choices on the major islands are as
great as your patience. First, if at all possible, package
your car rental with your airfare and accommodations.
Overnighter packages from Akamai Tours (971-3131 on
Oahu), Roberts Hawaii (945-2444), Island Getaways (922-
4400), or Hawaiian Overnighters (922-3444) give you a
round-trip fare between any two islands, a compact car
(and no mileage charge), and good-to-excellent accommodations for one night for about $90 plus tax per per-
son. Additional nights and days of car rental and accommodations are low, too, especially for better hotels and
resorts. The major airlines (and Hawaiian Airlines on
their mainland service) are using rental cars as a bonus
attraction, almost a giveaway, to get your airfare-hotel
package business. In a fly-drive deal with an airline,
which fluctuates too much these days to accurately pre-
dict, you shouldn't have to pay more than $25 per day or
$135 per week (without insurance) for a compact car.

For quick reference, the national/international and
statewide car rental agencies' mainland and Hawaii telephone numbers are:

American International: mainland, 800-527-0202;
Hawaii, 800-527-0160

Avis: mainland, 800-331-1212; Hawaii, 800-645-6393

Budget: mainland, 800-527-0700; Hawaii, 800-527-0707

Dollar: mainland, 800-367-7006

Hertz: mainland, 800-654-3131; Hawaii, 800-654-3001

National: mainland, 800-227-7368; Hawaii, 800-328-
6321

Thrifty: mainland, 800-331-4200; Hawaii, 800-331-9191

Holiday: mainland, 800-367-2631; Oahu, 836-1974

Tropical: mainland, 800-367-5140; Oahu, 836-1176

The national and statewide car rental agencies will split their car rental rates around the neighboring islands, letting you rent from one company for three weeks with at least 15 percent savings. This arrangement eliminates bargaining with local companies island-by-island for possibly lower rates, and the savings are guaranteed. During peak season and holiday periods, it's wise to book a car in advance, or you may be stuck without one. For the lowest rates, reserve a subcompact or compact with a stickshift and no air-conditioner, and then, when you arrive at the booking desk, ask politely if you can get an upgrade at the same price. This request actually may work.

Accommodations

Clean, comfortable, pleasant, well-located, and moderately priced accommodations are plentiful and easy to obtain on all the Hawaiian Islands—except Lanai. For only one or two people to have a dream vacation in Hawaii and spend less than $75 per day on accommodations, B&B accommodations are the best bet. There are only a few motels (in Lihue on Kauai and Waimea on the Big Island), only two official youth hostels (both in Honolulu), and a few cabins in state parks scattered around the state, some of them in the most superb locations like Wianapanapa State Park near Hana, Poli Poli Springs State Recreation Area in upcountry Maui, Hawaii Volcanoes National Park on the Big Island, and Kokee State Park on Kauai.

If you arrive in Oahu or on any other island without a reservation, the best source of hotel/condo information is the Hawaii Visitor's Bureau. Their free *Membership Accommodation Guide* is the most complete and up-to-date listing, including telephone numbers and addresses in all price ranges. When you look at accommodation prices, don't forget to add 9 percent room tax. Minimum stay requirements of three days are common, especially "in season"—December 15 to April 15.

B&B rooms range in price from $35 to $125 single or double. Even though county and local governments are resisting the growing trend, B&Bs are springing up on all the major islands. If they are not officially approved, B&Bs may not advertise themselves. Other B&B operators, however, will tell you about them. Check local newspapers, supermarket bulletin boards, and shopkeepers. But the most efficient way to find a wonderful variety of B&B bargains, hosts, and situations on all the islands is to contact: **Bed & Breakfast Hawaii**, toll-free 800-733-1632, Box 449, Kapaa, Kauai, HI 96746 (Kauai—822-7771, Maui—572-7692, Hawaii—959-9736); **Bed and Breakfast Pacific Hawaii**, 19 Kei Nani Place, Kailua, Oahu 96734 (262-6026 or toll-free 800-999-6026); **Go Native Hawaii**, 65 Halaulani Place, Hilo, HI 96721; and **B and B Maui Style**, P.O. Box 98, Puunene, HI 96784 (800-848-5567 or 879-7865).

Call Vickki Patterson at **Affordable Paradise B&Bs**, 362 Kailua Road, Kailua, HI 96734 (261-1693 or toll-free 800-925-9065) for a choice of over 300 hosts throughout the islands.

Camping

Hawaii offers some of the world's best camping and hiking. Hike shorelines, mountains, volcanoes, deserts, and jungle terrain, sometimes a mix in one day, and end the day at campsites that are easily accessible, near beautiful beaches, and surrounded by spectacular landscapes. Most camping is either free or costs a pittance. Some parks even offer the comfort of housekeeping cabins with all amenities, which must be reserved well in advance of your trip. The climate couldn't be better for camping and hiking in 2 national parks, 16 state parks, and 36 county parks open all year. Permits and reservations are required for public camping facilities. Island-by-island, *2 to 22 Days in Hawaii* points out the best camping spots and hiking trails. The State of Hawaii offers an excellent pamphlet on camping, picnicking, hiking, overnight cabins, and group accommodations. Write: State of Hawaii, Department of Land and Natural Resources, Division of State Parks, P.O. Box 621, Honolulu, HI 96809 (808-548-7455/56). For more detailed camping and hiking information, see Robert Smith's book, *Hawaii's Best Hiking Trails.*

What and How to Pack

You're allowed only three free bags, including one carry-on. Due to FAA pressure, airlines are strictly enforcing carryon baggage regulations. Carryons must fit under your seat or in an overhead compartment. Be sure to tag each bag with your name and hotel destination in Hawaii. Carry cosmetic essentials and a change of clothes with you, especially some beachwear, in case luggage is temporarily misrouted and delayed. If you do intend to use commuter flights, it's important to know that only two normal-sized bags, weighing up to 44 pounds, are free. A third bag or baggage over 44 pounds may be carried on board on a space-available basis only. Over 80 pounds, you may have to pay extra. Not so, however, for the big carriers. On flights from the mainland, your three bags can weigh 70 pounds each as long as the height, length, and width added together do not exceed 62 inches. Your carryon bag should be no more than 9 inches on one side to fit under the seat.

Travel as light as possible. When in doubt, leave it home. Arrange your travel wardrobe around two colors that allow you to mix and match tops and bottoms (pants, skirts, and shorts) for lots of variety with the fewest possible items. Plan to do laundry at least once and possibly twice a week to recycle your clothing. Pack jeans, shorts, loose-fitting shirts, and dresses (aloha shirts and muumuus await your shopping in Waikiki). Pack wrinkle-free and colorful clothing, dress shoes, walking and jogging shoes, and sandals. Hawaiians dress very casually, but bring one moderately dressy outfit for the rare nightlife or dining places that require it, if that's in your plan. Don't forget one very warm outfit, and strong but comfortable walking or hiking shoes for the trip up to Haleakala on Maui or Mauna Kea, Mauna Loa, and Hawaii Volcanoes National Park on the Big Island. Pack a sweater or jacket for cool days or evenings and trips in the mountains, a poncho for windward Hawaii and other windward island destinations, and a small, flat, empty bag for beach trips and shopping. Pack your cosmetics, shampoo, and other liquids in plastic bottles and place them in reclosable plastic bags to prevent leakage in unpressurized airplane baggage compartments. Take sunblock tanning lotion, your favorite moisturizer, a hat if you're sensitive to sun, sunglasses, and a bathing suit.

Recommended Reading

There are a few books that you might consider taking with you to supplement *2 to 22 Days in Hawaii.* For hikers, *Hawaii's Best Hiking Trails* by Robert Smith (Berkeley, Calif.: Wilderness Press, 1985) is a readable, well-organized guide, with everything you need to know about preparing for Hawaii's hiking trails.

My *Shopper's Guide to Arts and Crafts in the Hawaiian Islands* (Santa Fe, N.M.: John Muir Publications, 1990) tells all about the artists working on each island. It also includes additional suggestions for sightseeing, accommodations, and dining.

The University of Hawaii Press has produced full-color topographic maps for only $2.50 for each island. These detailed maps show every town, point of interest, type of road and trail, stream and waterfall, ridge and peak, and beach and park. These maps can be found in local bookstores.

For More Information

For informative brochures on all facets of life and sightseeing on the islands, visit or contact Hawaii Visitor's Bureau offices on the mainland or in Hawaii.

DAY 1 Fly from the U.S. mainland to Honolulu, Oahu, a 5-hour flight from the West Coast. Hawaii is two to five hours earlier than back home. Rent a car at the airport for the next three days unless you've decided to use TheBus. Waikiki has plenty of inexpensive and comfortable places to stay and eating places to match, especially for ethnic food lovers. Absorb the sunshine on a Waikiki beach or visit the marine wonders of Sea Life Park. Drive up to Diamond Head's crater for a superb panoramic view of Oahu's south coast. End the afternoon on Diamond Head or Koko Head and return to Waikiki for dinner and night-life, or sensibly retire for an early bedtime.

DAY 2 An ancient Hawaiian sacrificial site in the Punch-bowl Crater today is the National Memorial Cemetery of the Pacific and the profoundly contrasting start of a joyful trip over the Pali Highway to windward Oahu. Return to your accommodations, or consider staying on the wind-ward coast to continue to the North Shore tomorrow.

DAY 3 The North Shore is legendary for its surfing beaches—Sunset Point, Banzai Pipeline, and Waimea Bay. From Puu O Mahuka Heiau, an ancient temple, survey Waimea Bay. Visit the beautiful and informative Arboretum in Waimea Falls Park and have lunch in the park. Move on to the delightful and dynamic village of Haleiwa before returning to downtown Honolulu. Drive back through the pineapple fields of Wahiawa Plains, past Schofield Barracks (remember the movie *From Here to Eternity?*) and Pearl Harbor, with an optional stop at the USS *Arizona* Memorial. Before leaving Oahu, visit the Bishop Museum, the world's foremost collection of Pacific and Polynesian artifacts, art, and research. Take a walking tour of Honolulu's historic attractions. Your stroll through Old Honolulu ends in Merchant Street and Chinatown for a superb Chinese dinner.

DAY 4 Check out very early this morning for the flight to Maui. Rent a car at the airport and drive to the historic waterfront town of Lahaina, a fascinating and charming walking town and an ideal base for touring West Maui's coastline. After lunch, drive up the west coast and savor superb Kapalua Beach and visit Kaanapali and Kapalua resorts. After dinner in Lahaina, it's very early to bed for anyone planning to catch the sunrise on Haleakala's summit.

DAY 5 Try to rise at 3:00 a.m. to see an unforgettable sunrise from Haleakala volcano. (Or start out later in the morning and stay on the mountain for an awesome sunset.) Drive to the Puu Ulaula Visitor's Center at Haleakala's summit and then hike on Halemauu or Sliding Sands Trail. Afterward, tour one of the most beautiful, interesting, and overlooked parts of Hawaii—Upcountry.

DAY 6 Leave early for Hana Town. The incomparable (and much maligned) Hana Highway twists in and out of hundreds of switchbacks, with waterfalls in almost every gulch, dozens of narrow bridges, and bordering cliffs that drop off to pounding surf. Stop along the way at any of a number of magnificent scenic spots. In Hana, swim at Hamoa Beach and visit beautiful Helani Gardens. Have lunch and tour Hana and its outskirts. Decide whether to spend the next few hours on a scenic tour to Ohe'o Gulch, enjoy marvelous horseback riding on the Hana-Kaupo Coast, or just ease into relaxed Hana sightseeing. Plan to stay in Hana overnight.

DAY 7 On the drive back from Hana, stop off at the Keanae Arboretum. Drive to Kihei on the southwest coast by way of Paia and the Upcountry, with a stop for lunch. Your destination today is sun and surf at beautiful Makena Beach past Wailea resort and the Maui Prince resort, with an option of driving even farther to La Perouse Bay for sightseeing or snorkeling. Your relaxation is cut short by an afternoon flight to Molokai.

DAY 8 Spend the morning on an unforgettable mule ride or walk down to Kalaupapa, the former leper colony on land- and sea-locked Makanalua Peninsula. After a picnic lunch and tour of this historic peninsula, return to the trailhead at Kualapuu and drive to Palaau State Park. A recommended option is a drive to Waikolu Overlook for spectacular views of the valleys and pali below. Also consider a tour of the Kamakou Preserve to see hundreds of species of Hawaiian flora. Stay overnight near Kaunakakai.

DAY 9 The drive along the south shore to Halawa Valley at the eastern end of Molokai is as much a part of today's tour as visiting the famous valley itself. Stop at ancient fishponds and temple ruins, churches and other historic sites, and lovely small shady beaches inviting swims and relaxation. The hike to Moaula Falls in Halawa Valley takes more than two hours round-trip.Then drive to the opposite (western) end of the island, through Molokai Ranch, to tour Molokai Ranch Wildlife Park and explore beautiful Papohaku Beach.

DAY 10 Rise early to spend one very full day on nearby Lanai. (An alternative is to stay for one or more nights at one of the outstanding new resorts on Lanai.) After flying to Lanai, pick up your four-wheel drive, picnic supplies, a detailed trail map, and information on road conditions, and head for the Munro Trail. Drive up to The Hale, highest point on the island, for great views of the Hawaiian Islands. Drive down to Manele Road, leading to beautiful Manele and Hulopoe bays. Swim and/or snorkel at Hulopoe Bay. In the village of Kaunolu on the southwestern tip of Lanai are the remains of an important temple, Kamehameha's summer house, and other historical and legendary sites. Return to Molokai for the night.

DAY 11 Leave early for Hilo on the Big Island. Welcome to a profusion of blossom colors on the "Orchid Island" and the black lava and steaming fissures of the "Volcano Island." A counterclockwise exploration of these fascinating and contrasting sights starts in Hilo, whose 1940s appearance and pace make the transition from quiet Molokai and Lanai much easier. On a stroll through Hilo's historic downtown, you'll discover many old and beautiful wooden buildings with overhanging awnings to shelter you from possible rain. If this is a winter trip, prepare to be drenched occasionally by the same rain that makes Hilo a greenhouse of exotic tropical flowers. Visit the Lyman Mission House and Museum and other historic places before driving south a few miles to a local nursery with one of the largest collections of orchids in the state.

DAY 12 After visiting an early morning fish auction and another spectacular botanical garden, go back in time to the sugar plantation world of prewar Hawaii on the Hamakua Coast north of Hilo. Drive along Mamalahoa Highway, the old road bypassed by main Highway 19. On the way to Honokaa, you'll pass jungle canyons, each with hidden waterfalls cascading from lush steep slopes, and a handful of tiny plantation towns. A few miles north of Honokaa, home of the Hawaiian Holiday Macadamia Nut Factory, is one of the great adventures of the Hawaiian Islands, exploring Waipio Valley.

DAY 13 This morning explore Waimea and the town of Kamuela, the domain of one of the world's largest ranches, the 225,000-acre Parker Ranch. Leaving Waimea for north Kohala on Highway 250, once again you go back in time, this time to the plantation towns of Hawi and Kapaau. At the Pololu Valley Lookout, be slightly adventurous and walk down to the black sand beach. As an option, drive off the beaten track to find Kamehameha's birthplace, the ancient sacrificial temple Mookini Luakini Heiau, and the reconstruction of a 600-year-old fishing village.

DAY 14 From luxuriant forests and grassy upcountry rangeland, drive down to the hot and very dry lava shores of south Kohala. From a vision of Laurence Rockefeller, the Mauna Kea Beach Hotel grew out of this inhospitable coast filled with ancient temples, legends, and prophecies. After enjoying the hotel's magnificent beach and lunch, see some of the finest Hawaiian rock carvings at Puako and petroglyphs along the King's Highway footpath. Drive to a string of other resorts and gorgeous bays with perfect crescents of golden coral sand beaches (Anaehoomalu, Kaun'oa, and Hapuna), bordered by palms and delicate vegetation.

DAY 15 The sun-soaked region of jagged lava fields and tropical waters around the Kona Coast's major resort town, Kailua-Kona, still offers some of the same attractions that drew Hawaii's royal families here in another era. Links with this historic Hawaiian life-style can be seen throughout the town. In the afternoon, drive through hillsides thick with coffee trees producing famous Kona beans, to the Kealakekua Bay area and the white obelisk marking the spot where Captain Cook met his untimely death. Nearby is one of Hawaii's most fascinating historic sites, the Pu'uhonua O Honaunau National Historical Park, where priests in ancient Hawaii pardoned kapu (taboo) breakers. Return to Kailua-Kona for sunset, dinner, and local nightlife.

DAY 16 Drive south along Route 11—stopping at the old fishing village of Milolii—to the barren lava of Kau, to South Point, where Polynesian voyagers made their first landfall. After a side trip to the southernmost point in the United States and then Punaluu's black sand beach, you arrive at Hawaii Volcanoes National Park. Have dinner and stay overnight at Kilauea Lodge or at one of several excellent B&Bs in the area.

DAY 17 Return to the Visitor's Center to see a film on Hawaii's volcanic history and to get up-to-date information on today's trails and roads. Drive up Mauna Loa Strip Road to Bird Park for a picnic lunch and a walk through a densely forested bird sanctuary. Continue up the Strip Road to the overlook at the trailhead. Descend to the Kau Desert Footprints Trail. Afterward, at the Volcano Art Center, browse through an excellent collection of authentic Hawaiian arts and crafts housed in the original Volcano House.

DAY 18 From the Crater Rim Road, follow the Chain of Craters Road as far as you can drive toward the Wahaula Heiau, one of the island's first temples. Return to Crater Rim Road and Highway 11 to Keaau, and Highway 130 to the Puna Coast. Stop in the picturesque town of Pahoa for lunch and a stroll. Follow Route 132 to Kumukahi Lighthouse at Kapoho Point, where a huge lava flow miraculously parted around the lighthouse and closed again at the sea. Off Route 132, thousands of acres of lava flowed and hardened around an ohia forest. Today the skeletons of a fossilized ohia forest form part of lush Lava Tree State

Park. Tour the beautiful Puna Coast on Route 137. Return
to Pahoa where it is only 30 minutes to Hilo's Lyman Field
Airport for the flight to Lihue Airport on Kauai. Leave
enough time to visit a macadamia nut farm along Route 11.

DAY 19 On the way to an early trip up Waimea Canyon,
stop at the beautiful Ka'Imi Na'auao Hawaii Nei and
Hanapepe Canyon Lookout. Pass through Waimea, Captain
Cook's first landing place on Kauai. Lunch at the Kokee
Lodge Restaurant, in Kokee State Park, or picnic in the
adjoining meadow. Continue up to breathtaking Kalalau
Lookout, overlooking the Na Pali Cliffs to the blue ocean
thousands of feet below. Drive to accommodations, dinner,
and nightlife in the Poipu beach area.

DAY 20 Eat breakfast in Koloa Town, the state's first sugar
plantation, refurbished as a shopping area. Pick up a picnic
lunch in Koloa and return to Poipu to drive or walk to off-
the-beaten-track beaches for beachcombing, swimming,
and lunch. Tour in and around Poipu to see the Spouting
Horn blowhole and beautiful Kiahuna Gardens. Browse or
shop, especially among the stalls of jewelry vendors
around Spouting Horn.

DAY 21 Some of the state's most beautiful and hidden
beaches are found along the North Shore drive to Hanalei
Valley, only 50 miles from Poipu. Pass Hanalei, Lumahai,
and Haena. Picnic destination is the end of the road, Kee
Beach and the beginning of the Kalalau Trail. Spend the
evening in Hanalei.

DAY 22 Visit Wailua River State Park, the former home of
Hawaii's royalty, midway along the east coast, or visit
Grove Farm Homestead. Lunch somewhere between
Kapaa, Lihue, and the Kilohana Plantation, a beautifully
landscaped historic site and museum. If it's December
through March, this may be your last chance on this trip to
whale watch, which is an option from Lihue's waterfront.
After one of the best vacations in your life, it's time to
return to the U.S. mainland with an enviable collection of
photos and stories.

OAHU: HONOLULU AND WAIKIKI/ DIAMOND HEAD

After checking in at your accommodations, get some of Hawaii's wonderful sunshine and fresh air on the Diamond Head end of Waikiki. Pick up a plate lunch take-out for a picnic, cool off in the calm Waikiki waters, and then head for Diamond Head to get a great view of eastern Honolulu and Waikiki. Visit Sea Life Park and, afterward, find the right spot for sunset viewing.

Suggested Schedule

8:00 a.m.	Fly from U.S. mainland to Honolulu, Oahu.
12:00 noon	Arrive in Honolulu, and take a bus, limo, or rental car to your Waikiki accommodations.
1:00 p.m.	Snack lunch at Kapiolani Beach Park.
2:00 p.m.	Swim at Kuhio Beach Park or anywhere at the Diamond Head end of Waikiki, or drive to Diamond Head and climb to the summit.
3:30 p.m.	Head for Sea Life Park.
Sunset	Diamond Head or Koko Head.
7:00 p.m.	Return to accommodations for cleanup before dinner.
8:00 p.m.	Dinner in the Waikiki area.
10:00 p.m.	Enjoy some of Waikiki's nightlife.

Flying from the U.S. Mainland to Oahu
Most flights land at Honolulu International Airport. The flying time to Honolulu from Los Angeles is 5 to 6 hours. From Chicago, it's a 9-hour nonstop flight. One-stop from New York is about 11 hours in the air and a 13-hour trip. Return flights are slightly shorter.

Getting Around Oahu
From the Airport: The Honolulu Airport is about five miles west of Waikiki. It's a 20-minute drive except during rush hour, when it can take 45 minutes. Many hotels

have courtesy pickup, and their phones are near the baggage area. A taxi from the airport to Waikiki costs about $20 with tip depending on the distance and the number of bags. Call SIDA Taxis (836-0011) for the Honolulu area or Aloha State Taxi (847-3566) for elsewhere on the island. Better, use the Gray Line Airporter (834-1033) to Waikiki, Airport Motor Coach (926-4747), or Waikiki Airport Express (949-5249), all about $9 per person. Unfortunately, on the unbeatable TheBus, only a small carryon bag (not a backpack) that you can hold in your lap is allowed. Buses 8 and 20 pass just outside the airport and can take you to Ala Moana Terminal to pick up connecting buses.

TheBus: No matter where you go on Oahu, for a continuous trip in the same direction, TheBus costs only 60 cents (exact change only), free if you're under 6 or over 65. Transfers are free for a bus on a different line in the same direction, so you can get on and off free following this rule. You can do a complete circuit of the island, windward and leeward coasts, in about 4 hours on bus 52. Look for the bus painted yellow, brown, and orange, which has its main terminal at the Ala Moana Shopping Center on the Kona Street side of the ground-floor parking lot. At the information booth there, you can pick up maps and schedules, or call 942-3702. These are TheBuses to some of the primary destinations from the Ala Moana Terminal:

Airport: 8 and 20

Waikiki Beach: 2, 4, 8, 14, and 20

Arizona Memorial/Pearl Harbor: 20, 50, 51, and 52

Wahiawa, Honolulu downtown, and Chinatown: 1 through 9, 11, and 12

Hanauma Bay: 1 and 57

Sea Life Park: 57

Polynesian Cultural Center: 52

Queen Emma Palace: 4

Driving: Avoid driving during rush hours (7:00 to 9:00 a.m. and 4:00 to 6:00 p.m.) anywhere near Honolulu or the Pali roads. Buy a copy ($6.25) of *Bryan's Sectional Maps, Oahu*, which is indispensable for finding towns,

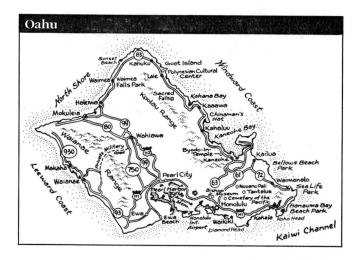

Oahu

subdivisions, park and recreation areas, shopping centers, and all attractions.

Car Rentals: Car rental prices may amaze you. For example, a Hertz subcompact (or even a compact if you are very nice) can be rented for $88 per week minus any discount such as AAA's 5 percent for members. If at all possible on Oahu, rent a car. You'll need it. The expensive part of car rental is the insurance, so leave home with adequate coverage to save $9 per day in Hawaii. Car rental agencies vary in their policies on renting without credit cards. Dollar, for example, will rent with a cash deposit, and Tropical requires a credit card. If it makes a difference to you, ask when you make a reservation. Always make a reservation at least a day ahead of time through the company's 800 number for the lowest rates. If you're going to rent cars on other islands, ask for an interisland rate. Even though you'll spend less than a week on any one island, you can piece together stays on all of the islands to get a weekly or monthly rate.

Local Oahu car rental numbers are Avis, 836-5531; Budget, 836-1700; Dollar Rent-A-Car, 926-4251; and Hertz, 836-2511; all are at the airport. National, 836-2655, is outside the airport. A phone call away, smaller firms offer slightly better deals. For older cars at bargain rates, call AAA Rents, 524-8060, or Alpert's Used Cars, 955-4370.

Other small local firms include Aloha Funway Rentals, 834-1016; Compact Rent-A-Car, 833-0059; Five-O Rent-A-Car, 836-1028; Holiday, 836-1974; Thrifty, 836-2388; Travelers Rent-A-Car, 833-3355; Tropical, 836-1041; and VIP Car Rental, 946-1671.

Bikes and Mopeds: Most sightseeing in the Honolulu area is within easy reach of bicycles or mopeds. The main problem with biking on Oahu is heavy traffic on the coastal roads. Rent a mountain bike to get off the main roads. Bikes at Aloha Funway Rentals are $10 per day. Mopeds at Funway are $14 for 24 hours. For more cycling information, contact Hawaii Bicycling League, Honolulu. Guided bicycle tours of Oahu and other islands are available through Island Bicycle Adventures, 569 Kapahulu Avenue, Honolulu, HI 96815, 732-7227, at costs of $90 to $120 per day including food and lodging.

Sightseeing Highlights

Kapiolani Beach Park—Named after King Kalakaua's wife, Queen Kapiolani, this park near the east end of Waikiki includes the world's largest saltwater swimming pool (War Memorial Natatorium), the Aquarium (923-9741, $2.50 donation per adult), the Honolulu Zoo (971-7171, 8:30 a.m. to 4:00 p.m. daily, adults $3, children 12 and under free), and a rose garden at Monsarrat and Paki avenues. Artists of Oahu/Sunday Exhibits, along the fence at the Honolulu Zoo, bring together a large number of the island's professional and part-time artists and craftspeople on Wednesdays and weekends between 10:00 a.m. and 4:00 p.m.

▲▲▲**Diamond Head**—This extinct volcano rising 760 feet above the east end of Waikiki can be reached by car from Monsarrat Avenue; then you can hike a half hour to the top. The crater got its name from British sailors in the early 1800s who found calcite crystals on the slopes and thought they were diamonds. Head to Kapiolani Park, then take Diamond Head Road and climb the kiawe-covered Kuilei Cliffs to the cliffside lighthouse. Beneath the cliffs are two parks you can walk down to: Diamond Head Beach Park and Kuilei Cliffs Beach Park, which has three turnouts. Stop at the second one.

Diamond Head Road descends between cliffside houses to Kahala Avenue and then climbs to the crater's east side. Pass through Fort Ruger (no longer operative) and down the crater's western slope on Monsarrat Avenue. At Diamond Head Road and 18th Street, take a left at a sign marked Civ-Alert USPFO and drive right into Diamond Head through a tunnel where the huge crater opens up to nothing more than the Hawaii National Guard Armory, the FAA's flight traffic control center, and many kiawe trees descended from a single seed planted by a priest 160 years ago. Your goal is the panoramic view from the crater's rim, reached by a 0.7-mile trail (one-way) up the northwest side of the crater. There are many lookout points along the way, as well as tunnels and bunkers, former gun emplacements, and towers. The observation point at the summit is an outstanding picnic spot.

▲▲**Koko Head and Koko Crater**—Travel along tree-shaded Kahala Avenue, past the Kahala Hilton to Kealaolu Avenue, then back to Kalanianaole Highway, through Henry J. Kaiser's 6,000-acre Hawaii Kai development to Koko Head Regional Park, scenic lookouts, and Koko Head Crater at 1,200 feet. On the crest of Koko Head is a side road that leads to a parking lot above picturesque Hanauma Bay, a volcanic crater opened to the ocean. Paths wind down the steep hillside to the coconut palm-fringed bay with tide pools, rocky headlands, and a pretty white sand beach. From one side of the lookout above Halona Blowhole, geysers shoot through the submerged lava tube. Halona Cove and Sandy Beach are especially nice places to have picnics.

▲▲**Sea Life Park**—Opposite Makapuu Beach Park, this park is worth visiting if only to see the 300,000-gallon Hawaiian Reef Tank, a three-story glass tank containing thousands of species of marine life. Also be sure to see the Ocean Science Theater's trained dolphins, sea lions, and penguins. It's open from 9:30 a.m. to 5:00 p.m. (10:00 p.m. on Thursday, Friday, and Sunday), adults $14.95, children 7 to 12 $8.50 and 4 to 6 $4.50. The Pacific Whaling Museum (free) just outside the entrance displays an outstanding collection of whaling artifacts.

Rising above the coastal highway are the 1,200-foot Makapuu Cliffs. Sea Life Park is at the base of these cliffs. The Kalanianaole Highway brings you through Waimanalo, past Waimanalo Beach, the longest stretch of sand on Oahu (site of the Robin Masters estate and the home of *Magnum P.I.*), to the junction of Highway 61, where you turn left onto the Pali Highway.

Where to Stay

Through one telephone call to the **Outrigger Hotels Hawaii** (800-733-7777), you can discuss a wide range of prices and rooms as close to the beach at budget prices as you can find in Waikiki.

    Outrigger Coral Seas Hotel, 250 Lewers Street, 923-3881, has appealing rooms, is decently decorated, with lanais, and is a stone's throw from the beach. Ask for a kitchenette. Off-season, rooms without kitchenettes are $65 to $85 and with kitchenettes $75 to $90 ($10 more in season). **Outrigger Waikiki Surf**, 2200 Kuhio Avenue, 923-7671, has renovated standard units without kitchenettes for $65 to $70 double and with kitchenettes for $70 to $75 off-season, $15 more during peak season. The newly refurbished **Outrigger Waikiki Surf East**, 420 Royal Hawaiian Avenue, 923-7671, has single and double rooms for $65 to $75, $5 more in peak season. Likewise, **Outrigger Waikiki Surf West**, 412 Lewers Street, 923-7671.

    If you can't find what you're looking for through Outrigger Hotels, contact **Aston Hotels and Resorts** (800-922-7866) and ask especially about the completely remodeled **Hawaiian Monarch**, 444 Niu Street, 949-3911, toll-free 800-535-0085, with rooms from $65 to $84 off-season without kitchenettes, $80 to $98 in season. Look on Beachwalk, the quiet little street that runs from Kalakaua down to the beach, for more of the best accommodation bargains in Waikiki. You can get a small one-bedroom apartment for $60 to $75, without tub or free local calls but right near the beach, at the **Niihau Apartment Hotel**, 247 Beachwalk, 922-1607. **Hawaiiana Hotel**, 260 Beachwalk, 923-3811 (800-367-5122), has 95

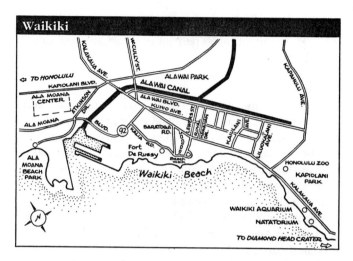

very simply furnished garden units with kitchens, situated around a beautiful tropical garden and two swimming pools. Complimentary breakfast, free parking, and washer/dryer are part of the $80 to $90 single, $85 to $95 double rates during the summer season (Apr. 20 to Dec. 17). Winter rates are only $5 higher. Parking is $6 per day in the rear of the hotel.

My favorite B&B belongs to charming **Paula Luv**, 3843 Lurline Drive, Honolulu, HI 96816, 737-8011, folk dancer, instructor, and Pacific region traveler. Atop Wilhelmina Rise with a magnificent view of Diamond Head and Honolulu, a room and private bath with a huge breakfast is only $35 per night.

Waikiki Circle Hotel, 2464 Kalakaua Avenue, 923-1571, right across from the beach with ocean views for most units, costs $47 to $62 with no kitchenettes. Mid-priced ($55-$70 per night) condo bargains that have any charm are not easy to find without the help of first-rate management companies. One of the best is Donald R. Blum's Waikiki Beach Condominiums, which can be contacted in California at 213-541-8813.

My favorite splurge stay, near Diamond Head on an 800-foot white sand beach, is the **Kahala Hilton**. The setting on Maunalua Bay is unsurpassed for an Oahu resort, and so are the restaurants (Maile, the Hala Terrace for breakfast, and the Royal Hula Buffet). Try to reduce the $180 per night by 50 percent in a package deal during off-season.

Where to Eat

The variety of inexpensive, ethnic, exotic, enjoyable, and outstanding restaurants in Waikiki compares with any city of its size in the world. When you travel to Oahu's beaches or mountaintops, or simply to the outskirts, take a picnic lunch from a restaurant. Here's a sampling. A local soup-to-nuts favorite (two locations, both open 24 hours) with good food, prices, and service is the **Wailana Coffee House**, 1860 Ala Moana Boulevard and 2211 Kuhio Avenue (Outrigger Malia Hotel). Both have validated parking.

Ono Hawaiian Foods, 726 Kapahulu Avenue, serves the real thing for your first, or umpteenth, genuine Hawaiian lunch or dinner. Nearby is **Keo's Thai Restaurant**, 625 Kapahulu; you can't go wrong here. The nondescript decor of **Chiang Mai** (2239 South King Street, 941-1151) is the opposite of Keo's (three) elegant dining spots, but they serve comparably delicious Thai food.

Hee Hing, 449 Kapahulu Avenue, Diamond Head Center, qualifies as Hawaii's best-decorated, best Cantonese restaurant, with the biggest menu and most reasonable prices. Other Chinese food favorites are **King Tsin** (1100 McCully, 946-3273), which serves the best Szechuan in town and, down the street, **The Mandarin** (942 McCully Street near Beretania, 946-3242), which serves delicious northern Chinese food. On the way out to Kahala, stop at **Yen King** in the Kahala Mall (732-5505) for a most complete and satisfying Chinese menu in all regional styles.

Don't miss at least one Japanese meal in Honolulu and Waikiki. **Kamigata** (Manoa Marketplace, 2756 Woodlawn Drive, near the University of Hawaii, 988-2107), beautifully decorated **Furusato** (Hyatt Regency Waikiki, 922-4991), and **Restaurant Suntory** (Third Floor, Building B, Royal Hawaiian Shopping Center, 922-5511) serve some of the best Japanese food you will find in Hawaii, à la carte. **Irifune** (563 Kapahulu Avenue, 737-1141) offers tasty teriyaki, tempura, stir-fried entrées, and other Japanese dishes, and has a very pleasant atmosphere. The sushi at tiny **Sushi Hirota** (3435 Waialae Avenue in Kaimuki, 735-5694), **Yanagi Sushi** (762 Kapiolani Blvd., 537-1525), and **Restaurant Sada** (1432 Makaloa St., behind Ala Moana Center, 949-0646) is as good as you'll find on Oahu. (Restaurant Suntory and Kamigata also have sushi bars.)

Greater Honolulu has quite a few excellent choices of Italian restaurants: **Sergio's** (445 Nohomani St., 926-3388) Italian specialties for lunch or dinner, weekdays only; **Baci's** delicious Italian dishes served in chic surroundings at the Waikiki Trade Center (2255 Kuhio Ave., 924-2533); **Che Pasta**, downtown (1001 Bishop St., 524-0004) and in Kaimuki (3571 Waialae Ave., 735-1777); and **Matteo's** calamari, veal, chicken, and other very tasty dishes served in quiet surroundings until midnight in the Marine Surf Hotel (364 Seaside Ave., 922-5551).

Nightlife

Rascals, 2301 Kuhio Mall, 2nd floor, 922-5566, has multi-level disco until 4:00 a.m. The **Red Lion Dance Palace**'s disco-video system also keeps the dance floor crowded until 4:00 a.m., at 240 Lewers Street; the **Blue Water Seafood**, 2350 Kuhio Avenue (926-2191), has disco-videos; **Garden Bar** and **La Mex** in the Royal Hawaiian Shopping Center, 926-2000, offer entertainment nightly. You can listen to ukulele music from 9:00 p.m. to midnight on Sunday nights at **Buzz's Original Steak House** (2535 Coyne St., 944-9781). Or try low-key guitar playing at the **Seafood Emporium**, 2201 Kala Kaua, Wednesday through Sunday nights, 922-5547; **Trader Vic's**, daily, 923-1581; **Hawaiian Regent Hotel**, 922-6611, video dancing with two dance floors, until 4:00 a.m.; **Hyatt Regency Waikiki**, 922-9292, at **Harry's Bar**, **Trappers**, and especially disco at **Spats** until 4:00 a.m. nightly; the **Jazz Cellar**, 205 Lewers Street, 923-9952, with live rock and jazz until 4:00 a.m.; **Sheraton Moana Hotel**, 922-

3111; and **Sheraton Princess Haiulani**, 922-5811, with nightly entertainment.

   Robert and Roland Cazimero (The Brothers Cazimero) and their hula dancers perform in the Monarch Room of the Royal Hawaiian Hotel, Waikiki (923-7311), Tuesday to Saturday. **Danny Kaleikini**, hula dancers, and other musicians are at the Kahala Hilton Hotel (734-2211). For a very memorable experience, see the imu ceremony, torchlighting ritual, beachfront huki-lau (communal net fishing), Polynesian review, arts and crafts display and luau at **Paradise Cove Luau** (973-5828). Another outstanding cultural dance show is provided by dancers from Fiji, Samoa, New Zealand, and Tahiti at the **Ainahau Showroom**, Sheraton Princess Jaiulani Hotel, Waikiki (922-5811). The **Sea Life Park Hawaiian Revue** (259-7933), a Polynesian show, performs on Thursdays and Sundays at 8:30 p.m. The cost is included in park admission. **Kumu Kahua Theater Company** produces plays about Hawaii on the grounds of St. Andrews Cathedral (224 St. Emma Square, 599-1503). The **John F. Kennedy Theater**, University of Hawaii-Manoa (948-7655), produces Chinese opera, Kanuki, Noh plays, and also American musicals.

   For up-to-date choices and information, consult the free *This Week in Oahu*, a valuable guidebook found at all hotels.

Itinerary Options
Beaches: Greater Honolulu has one pretty beach at Diamond Head Beach Park, directly below the crater and backed by cliffs. Snorkeling is good but swimming isn't, and the park usually swarms with tourists and, on weekends, locals. For very pretty and superb beaches that rival those on other islands, spend some time on the windward coast, especially in the Kailua, Lanikai, and Laie areas.

   Cruises: See free local tourist magazines to clip discount coupons for dinner cruises. Most depart from the Kewalo Basin Marina, near Fisherman's Wharf, about 6:30 p.m. and return at 8:30 p.m., for $35 to $50 per person.

Pearl Harbor cruises and sunset cruises and Waikiki-Diamond Head cruises are offered by Hawaiian Cruises Ltd., 923-2061; sunset and dinner cruises can be arranged with Windjammer Cruises, 521-0036.

Gliders, planes, and helicopters: The least expensive, most thrilling and serene way to see the island from the air is in a glider. Drive out to the east coast past Haleiwa and Mokuleia to Dillingham Air Force Base, where the Honolulu Soaring Club (677-3434) offers 20-minute one- or two-passenger piloted glider rides for $40 to $60 from 10:30 a.m. to 5:30 p.m. daily. Half-hour plane rides for only $30 and an hour for $50, in Cessna 172s or 206s, are available from Surf Air Tours, 637-7003. Helicopter tours around the island range from $40 quickies over Waikiki to tours of Oahu for $200 or more per person. Contact Hawaii Pacific Helicopters, 836-2071; Kenai Air Hawaii, 836-2071; and Royal Helicopters, 941-4683.

Bicycling: Check with the Hawaii Bicycling League (988-7175) for bike rides that fit your condition. Otherwise, bike through Kahala to Hanauma Bay, drive out Route 83 to Kaneohe Bay and head north to Laie, or drive out to Haleiwa and bike north along the North Shore or west on Route 930 to Mokuleia Beach.

Tennis: Kapiolani Tennis Courts (4, lighted); Ilikai Hotel (5 courts, 7:00 a.m. to 5:00 p.m., 949-3811); and the Turtle Bay Hilton & Country Club (293-8811).

Windsurfing: Kailua Beach Park and Windsurfing Hawaii (261-3539) for gear and instruction; Diamond Head Beach Park and Aloha Windsurfing (926-1185) for gear and instruction.

Game fishing: The waters offshore Oahu are full of ahi, ono, opakapaka, aku, mahi mahi, au, and marlin. The fishing charters moor at Kewalo Basin and include Island Charters (536-1555) and Coreene-C's Charters (536-7472); Kono, 531-0060; and Sport Fishing Hawaii, 536-6577.

Snorkeling and scuba diving: Both beginners and experienced divers have many choices around Oahu. Hanauma Bay (early in the morning) and Sans Souci

Beach are best for novice divers and snorkelers. More
experienced divers will try Manana Island, Makapuu
Point, Fantasy Reef (off Waialae Beach at Kahala), Laie
Beach (between Laie and Laniloa Point), and Haleiwa
Beach. In summer (not in winter), experienced snorkel-
ers will find a friendly assortment of fish at Black Point,
Waimea Beach, Sunset Beach, Pupukea Bay Beach, Kahe
Beach Park, and Nanakuli Beach Park. For diving equip-
ment rental, contact the Leeward Dive Center (696-3414)
for Waianae Coast diving; Dan's Dive Shop, 536-6181,
next to Little George's restaurant on Ala Moana
Boulevard, for diving excursions, gear, and instruction; or
Waikiki Diving in two locations, 420 Nahua and 1734
Kalakua, 922-7188. For snorkeling equipment rental, con-
tact Fort DeRussy Beach Services, 949-3469; South Sea
Aquatics, 538-3854; or Blue Water Snorkel, 926-4485.

Surfing: Body-surf at Makapuu Beach beyond Koko
Head beaches, Diamond Head end of Prince and Kuhio
beaches, and Kalama Beach (Kailua) between Kalaka
Place and Kaiona Place. Board-surf at Waikiki Beach, Ala
Moana Beach, Diamond Head Beach, Haleiwa Beach
Park, Barbers Point, Chun's Reef, Pupukea, Banzai
Pipeline, Kalama Beach, Makaha Beach, Yokohama
Beach, Sunset Beach, Ehukai Beach Park, and Waimea
Beach Park. Contact Local Motion Surfboards, 944-8515;
Waikiki Beach Services, 923-3111; and the Haleiwa Surf
Center, 637-5051.

Horseback riding: The two best areas for sightseeing
by horseback are out of resorts. The Sheraton Makaha
Resort, 695-9511, has rides up into the back reaches of
Waianae's Makaha Valley; and the Turtle Bay Hilton, 293-
8811, has trails along the beautiful palm and ironwood
groves of deserted beaches on the northwest Kahuku tip.
Kualoa Ranch has rides for $20 per hour, $30 for two
hours, 237-8515.

Camping is permitted at three state campgrounds:
Keaiwa Heiau State Park; Malaekahana State Park (sup-
plemented by housekeeping cabins), on a beautiful white
sandy beach on the east coast; and the Sand Island State
Campground in Honolulu Harbor. At Bellows Field

Beach Park, only on weekends, near the ironwoods that ring the beach, you can camp with a permit that you have to obtain in person from the Department of Land and Natural Resources, Division of State Parks, 1151 Punchbowl Street, Room 310, Honolulu HI 96813, 548-7455.

At Malaekahana State Recreation Area, tent camping (with a county permit) is idyllic, and you can carry your gear over to Goat Island for unofficial camping. Kahana Bay Beach Park has a white sand beach that is excellent for camping (county permit) and a 5-mile hiking trail into Kahana Valley State Park. Mokuleia Beach has long unpopulated sections that are popular with unofficial campers. Keaiwa Heiau State Recreation Area in the Koolau foothills is surrounded by a forest with a network of trails. (Route 90 west to Aiea, Aiea Heights Drive mauka to the park.) There's a five-day limit and no camping on Wednesdays or Thursdays. Contact Department of Land and Natural Resources, Division of State Parks, 548-7455. Camping is permitted at 15 county beach parks, Fridays through Wednesdays. Other excellent campgrounds are at Kahe, Kahuna Bay, Keaau, Luaualei, Nanakuli, Punaluu, and Swanzy.

Tantalus and Makiki Valley trails: From Honolulu it is three miles to Makiki Valley and six miles to Tantalus Drive. Puu Ohia, the highest peak of Tantalus, is the place from which to reach many of the area's best hiking trails, none of which are too difficult and all of which reveal magnificent natural beauty.

OAHU: PALI DRIVE AND WINDWARD COAST

Leave Waikiki for the windward coast's marvelous beaches and unusual parks and the Polynesian Cultural Center. Up over the Nuuanu Pali, with cliffs created by winds from the east and valleys like Nuuanu cut by streams from the west, to the windward side, you'll pass the Royal Mausoleum, Queen Emma's Summer Palace, and the Pali itself, where Kamehameha drove 16,000 enemy warriors to their deaths in his final victory to control the islands. Excellent beach parks line the windward shore.

Suggested Schedule

7:00 a.m.	Breakfast, swim, or jog on the beach.
8:30 a.m.	Drive to the Punchbowl.
9:30 a.m.	Drive up Pali Highway to Queen Emma's Summer Palace.
11:00 a.m.	Nuuanu Pali Lookout and some refreshments.
11:45 a.m.	Stop at Haiku Gardens.
12:30 p.m.	Tour the Valley of the Temples.
1:15 p.m.	Drive north on Highway 83 along the windward coast to Heeia State Park or Malaekahana Bay for a picnic lunch.
2:45 p.m.	Visit the Polynesian Cultural Center.
3:00 p.m.	See the "Pageant of the Long Canoes," followed by the Pacific Island Exhibits.
7:00 p.m.	See "This Is Polynesia" dinner show.

Orientation

Lunalilo Highway (H1) runs north-south through Honolulu along the base of five major ridges, including Makiki Heights with Tantalus Drive, and five valleys, including Nuuanu Valley that flattens out to become the downtown. The Pali Highway (61) and Likelike Highway run from H1 through these valleys between ridges to Kam Highway (83) on the windward side.

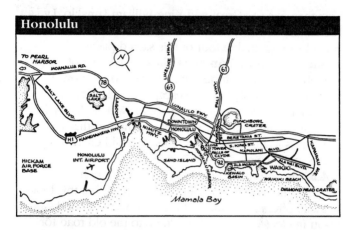

Honolulu

Sightseeing Highlights

▲▲▲**The Pali Highway**—Highway 61 through Nuuanu
Valley cuts across Oahu from Honolulu to the windward
coast, passing a series of the region's outstanding sightseeing attractions. The off-ramp into Nuuanu Valley passes Queen Emma's Summer Palace, the royal retreat in
lush highlands in the last 1800s and now a museum.
Before the breathtaking overlook, turn onto Nuuanu Pali
Drive, which winds back to the highway.

▲▲**The Punchbowl and the Royal Mausoleum**—The
National Memorial Cemetery of the Pacific is on the 112-
acre floor of a long-extinct volcano. The almost perfectly
round Punchbowl Crater was called Puowaina (Hill of
Sacrifice) by the ancient Hawaiians. At the top of
Puowaina Drive at 2177 Puowaina Drive, 546-3190, the
Punchbowl is open 8:00 a.m. to 5:30 p.m. daily October
through March, 8:00 a.m. to 6:30 p.m. March through
September. Take a moment to reflect on the price of war:
more than 30,000 service people are buried here, and
over 26,000 are listed as missing in action. The lookout at
the top of the crater offers a great view of Honolulu. To
get there, take Punchbowl Avenue where it crosses King,
go under the freeway, and watch for signs to Punchbowl
Memorial. Take a right on Puowaina Street into the
crater.

▲**The Royal Mausoleum** contains the final resting place
of every modern Hawaiian king and queen except King

Kamehameha the Great and King William Lunalilo. Lydia Namahana Maioho, curator, and her son, William, will provide a memorable tour of this sacred place.

▲**Queen Emma's Summer Palace**—The wife of Kamehameha IV built her white frame house, now a museum, in the cool hills to escape the summer heat. This area was Honolulu's first suburb. Watch closely for the Pali Highway turnoff sign on the right so that you don't miss it. Admission $4 adults, $1 children 12-18, opens at 9:00 a.m., 595-3167, 2913 Pali Highway.

▲▲▲**The Nuuanu Pali Lookout**—You may have watched the sunset from here last evening, but this lookout also offers a magnificent morning view of windward Oahu in clear weather. Walk down to the old road for even better views.

▲**Haiku Gardens**—A former favorite getaway place for ancient Hawaiians, in the mid-1800s, the 16-acre site known today as Haiku Gardens (46-316 Haiku Rd.) was deeded to an Englishman by Hawaiian alii. Acres of exotic plants, streams, picturesque lily and tropical fish ponds, bamboo groves, and huge banyan trees are the foreground for spectacular Koolau cliffs rising up from the dense foliage. On Saturdays, a thatched-roof hut tucked into the tropical vegetation has a succession of weddings. A Chart House restaurant (247-6671) now overlooks the pali cliffs and garden.

▲**The Valley of the Temples Memorial Park**—In Kaneohe, turn onto Kahekili Highway (83) to the entrance (47-200 Kahekili Highway, 239-8811) to a perfect setting for a universal faith cemetery. Set in a classic Japanese garden with swans and peacocks, the centerpiece of the park is the ornate Buddhist Byodo-In Temple (Temple of Equality), a replica of the famous 900-year-old Byodo-In Temple of Kyoto. From the pagoda (Meditation House) at the top of the hill is the best view of the grounds ($2 admission for adults, $1 for those under 12, and $1 for those over 55).

▲**The Polynesian Cultural Center**—Laie is the center of the Mormon church in Hawaii. Starting in 1963, the Church of Jesus Christ of the Latter Day Saints packaged

Polynesia into a highly successful theme park that really is a unique educational experience worth its stiff price.

The core of the 42-acre PCC is its seven re-created villages: six Polynesian and one Melanesian—Hawaii, Samoa, Tonga, the Marquesas, Fiji, New Zealand, and Tahiti. Each village displays excellent craftsmanship in construction and handicrafts native to the particular cultural homeland. Guides native to each island explain the cultural background of the homeland and talk about the foods and handcrafts exhibited. Walk, take a shuttle tram, or tour the area by canoe over artesian-fed waterways.

"This Is Polynesia," the very exciting and moving 90-minute dinner show of music, dance, and historical drama, begins at 7:30. An all-you-can-eat dinner is served at the center's Gateway Restaurant. At the end of the day, after the buffet dinner, a 70-foot by 130-foot-wide screen in a new theater shows a 40-minute adventure film about the Pacific region.

Packages ranging from $40 to $72 buy different combinations of entertainment and meals in addition to the seven Polynesian villages, craft, hula and other demonstrations from 12:30 to 9:00 p.m. Book round-trip transportation for about $12 per adult. Better still, incorporate an all afternoon and evening trip to the PCC with an all morning excursion from Honolulu to Laie. Watch for special discounts that may be offered by tour operators or advertised in *This Week in Oahu.*

Where to Stay

The reef in front of Halehaha Beach, in windward Hauula, before you reach Laie, shelters a shoreline with condominium units, **Pat's at Punaluu** (53-567 Kamehameha Hwy., Hauula, 293-8111). The 30 to 40 units for rent in this building (and others with permanent residents) start at $65. There is a swimming pool, a sauna, a gym, and the popular Pat's at Punaluu restaurant (293-8502) where you can get breakfast, lunch, and dinner. About halfway between the Paniolo and Pat's, a tradition for budget travelers, is Margaret Neal's **Countryside Cabins** (53-224 Kam Highway, Hauula HI 96717, 237-8169). It is simply

announced by an easily missed white sign that says
Cabins. Clean but "rustic" studios are $40 a night and
$190 a week, in one of Oahu's prettiest coastal areas.

Wendy Judy's **Akamai B&B** (263-0227) offers two
large studios, with a pool and near the beach for $69 per
night or $380 per week, with special rates for seniors.
Minimum stay is three nights. If Judy's is full, she'll fix
you up at one of 26 other B&Bs.

Drive on Highway 61 through Kailua to Kalaheo
Avenue that runs along the coast. Pat O'Malley's **Pat's
Kailua Beach Properties**, 204 S. Kalaheo Avenue,
Kailua, HI 96734, 261-1653, offers about 20 furnished cottages in a beautiful setting overlooking Kailua Beach
which cost from $60 to $80 per day. (About 20 more of
Pat's cottages and houses cost more to rent.) Drive
another 10 miles north on Highway 83 to Laie and stay
overnight for $75 to $85 at the **Laniloa Lodge Hotel**, 55-
109 Laniloa Street, Laie, 293-9282 or toll-free 800-526-
4562, next to the Polynesian Cultural Center. This is an
excellent base for visiting Waimea Bay and Haleiwa
attractions along with the Polynesian Cultural Center.

Where to Eat
The Windward Mall Shopping Center in Kaneohe, like
Ala Moana Shopping Center, provides most of the inex-
pensive eating that you'll need in this part of the island.
The **Yummy Korea BBQ, Deli Express, Taco Shop,
Cinnabon's** cinnamon rolls, **Harpo's** excellent deep-
dish pizza, **Patti's Chinese Kitchen**, and **Little Tokyo**
offer variety and filling portions.

If half-pound hamburgers and beer in 16-ounce mason
jars are not especially to your liking, skip **Paniolo Cafe**
(53-146 Kam Highway, Hauula, 237-8521) and move on
to **Pat's at Punaluu** (53-567 Kamehameha Highway, 293-
8502) for Kahuku shrimp curry and guava-glazed lamb.

From the Polynesian Cultural Center the road continues through the village of Kahuku and past Kahuku
Sugar Mill (293-2444). Since this is the midpoint of the
circle-the-island tour, a visit to the **Country Kitchen
Restaurant** (293-2414) would make sense. The interior is

much nicer than the outside suggests. The menu offers all three meals any time of day, 8:00 a.m. to 9:00 p.m. seven days a week. The special—old-fashioned calico bean soup—is worth the drive.

The big decision of the day is whether to eat lunch at the Country Kitchen or wait a few minutes for the famous homegrown shrimp at **Amorient Aquafarm**, a roadside stand next to their own 175-acre shrimp and fish farm, one-acre ponds that you can see from the highway and the stand. Open 10:00 a.m. to 5:30 p.m. Solve the dilemma by taking cooked shrimp tempura, cooked shrimp tails, or shrimp cocktail with you. (Chances are you'll never get farther than your car.)

Itinerary Options

After leaving the Byodo-In Temple, continue on Kam Highway past Kaneohe to **Heeia State Park**, an ideal picnic site on a beautiful small peninsula overlooking Heeia Fishpond, one of the few left on the island and the largest.

On Saturday and Sunday, from 10:00 a.m. to 3:00 p.m., art enthusiasts can have one of the rarest treats in all of Hawaii: a visit to the serene and beautiful gardens, gallery, and home of **Hiroshi Tagami and Michael Powell** (239-8146). The galleries, arranged in interconnected Japanese-style buildings and rooms with the gentle sound of water flowing in small courtyards, contain sculptures, pottery, and a limited amount of the art of Tagami and Powell.

In a lush 725-acre setting, **Senator Fong's Plantation and Gardens** in Eisenhower Valley contains the visitors center; Kennedy orchards and 75 varieties of edible trees and plants; Nixon Valley, traditional ethnic gardens (Japanese, Chinese, Filipino, and Hawaiian); and Ford Plateau, a pine garden. After a three-mile, 40-minute guided mini-bus tour (10:30 a.m., 11:30 a.m., 1:00 and 2:00 p.m.) of Senator Fong's Plantation and Gardens ($6.50 adults, $3 children 5-12, under 5 free, 47-285 Pulama Road, a mile from the junction of route 83 and Kahekili Highway, 239-6775), you can return to Honolulu

on the Likelike Highway (Route 63) via the Wilson
Tunnel, or continue along Kaneohe Bay past fertile
Waiahole and Waikane valleys.

Large schools of delicious *akule* (big-eyed scad) visit
Kahana Bay about 15 miles north of Kaneohe. Hawaiians
living in the valley built shrines on bluffs surrounding the
bay and the fishponds. Kahana Bay County Park has
camping (county permit), picnic, and other facilities and
good swimming and bodysurfing. Across the road in
Kahana Valley State Park, a five-mile trail past old
Hawaiian farms winds deep into **Kahana Valley**.

Just south of the village of Hauula, a clear pool at the
base of an 80-foot waterfall awaits travelers determined
to hike 2.2 miles up a rough trail (treacherous when
muddy after rains) through dense vegetation for about an
hour to **Sacred Falls**.

Pounders Beach (appropriately named for its pounding surf) near the Polynesian Cultural Center is privately
owned but open to the public and has no facilities. The
mile-long beach in the armpit of **Laie Point**, reached by
a stairway down the rocks through a right-of-way halfway up the peninsula, is one of the liveliest in Hawaii.
Midway down the beach, look for an opening in the
coral for extended, protected swimming and snorkeling.
Shade trees make picnicking perfect on this beach.

Malaekahana State Recreation Area is one of the
island's prettiest parks. For campers, this beach should be
the choice destination along the Windward Coast, insulated from the highway by shade trees, with the joyful
bonus of wading over to **Mokuauia Island (Goat
Island)**, in water shallow on calm days and waist high
on others. The white sand beach on the leeward side of
this bird refuge is a dream South Pacific getaway.

OAHU: NORTH SHORE TO DOWNTOWN HONOLULU

The North Shore is world famous for its legendary surfing beaches. In the winter, gaze in awe at Sunset, Ehukai, and Banzai beaches and Waimea Bay (calm as a lake in summer). Drive up Pupukea Road for the spectacular view of the North Shore from Puu O Mahuka Heiau. Visit beautiful Waimea Falls Park. After lunch in Haleiwa or on Mokuleia Beach, return to downtown Honolulu with a brief stop at the Wahiawa Botanic Garden. Spend the rest of the afternoon exploring historic and restored sections of Honolulu before dinner in Chinatown.

Suggested Schedule

7:00 a.m.	Swim before breakfast?
8:00 a.m.	Breakfast and depart for North Shore.
10:00 a.m.	Waimea Falls Park or farther north to surfing beaches.
12:00 noon	Lunch at Proud Peacock in Waimea Falls Park or in Haleiwa.
1:00 p.m.	Drive on Highway 99 through the pineapple and sugarcane fields to Honolulu.
1:30 p.m.	Explore the Bishop Museum.
3:30 p.m.	Brief look at Aliiolani Hale, Iolani Palace, Washington Place, St. Andrews Cathedral, Kawaiahao Church, the Mission Houses Museum and its excellent gift shop.
4:30 p.m.	Visit the Hawaii Maritime Center and watch the sunset over Honolulu from Aloha Tower.
6:30 p.m.	Dinner in Chinatown.
8:00 p.m.	Another swing through Waikiki's nightlife.

Sightseeing Highlights
▲**Sunset, Ehukai, Banzai Pipeline, and Waimea Bay—** Surfing beaches here, for experts only from November through February, are fairly safe for swimming at other times of year.

▲**Puu O Mahuka (Hill of Escape) Heiau**—Sited above
Waimea Park, this spiritually significant and most famous
temple of Oahu probably was the site of human sacrifices in the precolonization period. The view of Waimea
Bay is outstanding.

▲▲▲**Waimea Falls Park**—This is a privately owned
1,800-acre nature reserve. The entrance is several miles
into a lush valley that was once inhabited by thousands
of Hawaiians. Primarily a botanical garden, the park
includes entertainment such as hula dancers and divers
who plunge 55 feet into the pool below the falls. You
can swim at the base of the falls, walk on beautiful trails,
or just stroll around the central meadow's Waimea
Arboretum and Botanical Gardens with or without a free
guided tour. You'll also see some species of Hawaiian
wildlife including nene geese, "Kona nightingales" (wild
donkeys), and wild boar. For visitors to the islands,
admission charges are $14.95 for adults, $7.95 for children 7 to 12, and $2.25 for children 4 to 6. The park is
open from 10:00 a.m. to 5:30 p.m. (638-8511 or 923-
8448). On weekends, the park can be quite crowded, but
trails up the hillsides offer an escape. Ride the open-air
tram to the top of the valley and walk down. Spend the
whole day, if possible, and during full moon take a
moonlight walk before dining at the Proud Peacock
restaurant (closes at 9:00 p.m.).

▲**Haleiwa**—Amazingly, Haleiwa (house of the frigate
bird) is the only town or village along Oahu's entire
coastline that preserves any of its original quaint rural
charm, today combined with boutiques, gift shops, and
art galleries. The down-home country atmosphere is still
preserved in neighboring Waialua, an old plantation
town where R. Fujioka & Sons Ltd. has run a grocery
store next to twin gas pumps for fifty years, and the local
bank is now the Sugar Bar and Restaurant.

▲**Dole Pineapple Pavilion**—Route 930-80 from
Mokoleia and Route 82 from Haleiwa rise through end-
less rows of pineapples up the 1,000-foot Leilehua
Plateau toward Wahiawa and split again into Kam
Highway and Kaukonahua Highway (Route 99). James

Dole started his first cannery for pineapples in 1899, and, not far from Wahiawa, the Dole Pineapple Pavilion demonstrates the canning process from 9:00 a.m. to 6:00 p.m. daily. A little farther toward Wahiawa, Del Monte displays 20 kinds of bromeliads, the botanic name for pineapples.

▲▲▲**Bishop Museum**—This museum at 1525 Bernice Street, 847-3511, contains the most complete collection of historical displays on Hawaii and Polynesia in the world. Be sure to see the Hall of Hawaiian Natural History. Admission is $7 for adults and $4.95 for children 6-17. Museum hours: 9:00 a.m. to 5:00 p.m. Monday through Saturday and the first Sunday of every month, Family Sunday, with food booths, craft displays, and entertainment. To get there, take exit 20A off H1 to Route 63. Quickly get into the right lane for a right turn on Bernice Street. Or, bus 2 lets you off two blocks from the museum on Kapalama Street.

▲**Downtown Honolulu**—King Kamehameha's statue here is one of three. In front of the Aliiolani Hale, it is a duplicate made to replace the original, which was lost at sea en route from Paris. It was found much later in a Port Stanley junkyard and erected in Kapaau not far from the king's birthplace. Aliiolani Hale (the Judiciary Building), at King and Mililani streets, was supposed to be a palace, but Kamehameha V, who commissioned it, died before its completion, and it was converted to a court building. Iolani Palace was completed in 1882 and used as a royal palace for only 17 years. To the left of Washington Place is St. Andrews Cathedral, built in 1867 of stone shipped from England. In front is the Hawaii State Capitol. Kawaiahao Church, at South King and Punchbowl streets, was built in 1841 out of coral quarried from local reefs. The Mission Houses Museum on King Street across from the church includes the oldest wooden structure in Hawaii, precut and shipped from Boston in 1819, as well as the first printing press west of the Rockies. It's open daily and charges $5 for adults, $3 for children 6-15. The gift shop has an excellent collection of Hawaiiana. The museum also offers a two-hour walking tour of Honolulu.

▲**The Hawaiian Maritime Center** consists of three
attractions. Aloha Tower on Pier 9, at ten stories the tallest
building in town when it was built in 1926, still commands
excellent views of the harbor and city. The *Falls of Clyde*
on Pier 7, built in Scotland in 1878, is the world's only full-
rigged, four-masted ship. The *Hokuke'a*, an authentic replica of an ancient Polynesian double-hulled sailing canoe,
made a 5,000-mile round-trip to Tahiti in 1976. Open daily
9:00 a.m. to 5:00 p.m., $7 for adults, $4 for ages 6 to 17,
under 6 free (536-6373).

▲**Chinatown**—On the eastern fringe of downtown
between Nuuanu Avenue, North Beretania Street, and
South King Street, this part of town is both modern and
rundown (the whole district burned down in 1900). The
pagoda of Wo Fat's at the corner of Hotel and Maunakea
streets is a good starting point for a tour. The most interesting stores are on Maunakea Street between Hotel and
King streets: little Chinese groceries, herb shops dispens-
ing ancient medications like ground snakeskin and pow-
dered monkey brain, jewelry shops, ceramic shops,
acupuncture supplies, and import stores. Also note the art
galleries on Nuuanu, Smith, and Maunakea streets. Try a
piece of lotus root candy. The island end of Maunakea
Street is bounded by the Cultural Plaza, designed to exhibit Hawaii's multicultural makeup. Nearby is the People's
Open Market, a cooperative of open-air stalls.

Where to Eat
North Shore
The **Proud Peacock** in Waimea Falls Park is a very special
place to have lunch or dinner surrounded by gardens,
with peacocks roaming about.

Enjoy breakfast at the **Coffee Gallery** in the North
Shore Center or at the **Cafe Haleiwa**, 66-460 Kamehameha
Highway, 637-5561, a tiny place across from the post
office on the left as you enter Haleiwa, which serves
excellent and cheap breakfasts with names like "Surf Rat"
and "Dawn Patrol," in honor of the cafe's hungry apres-
surfing clientele. Sunday brunch (10:00 a.m.-3:00 p.m.) is
the best way to start Sunday on the North Shore. For

lunch and dinner, there are several very good choices.
Jameson's By the Sea (62-540 Kam Highway, 637-4336)
serves stuffed shrimp, mahi mahi, catch of the day, and a
variety of other lunch and dinner fare. The deck facing
the ocean is the place to be at any time of day. Several
eating places in the Haleiwa Shopping Plaza serving food
ranging from sashimi to steamer clams: **Steamer's** (637-
5971); Cal-Mex specialties at **Rosy's Cantina** (637-3538);
better than average pizza at **Pizza Bob's** (637-5095);
chicken ribs and burgers grilled Hawaiian-style over
kiawe wood at **Kiawe-Q** (637-3502). **Kua Aina
Sandwich Shop** may or may not have the best hamburgers on the island, but they look like the biggest.

Across Route 99 from Schofield Barracks, made infa-
mous in James Jones's *From Here to Eternity*, **Kemoo
Farm** (621-8481) on the shore of Lake Wilson provides a
lunch and dinner (except Monday) hearty enough to satisfy GIs, locals, and tourists.

Honolulu

In 1986, **Wo Fat's**, 115 Hotel Street, 537-6260, celebrated
its 100th anniversary as Honolulu's premier Chinese
restaurant. **Sea Fortune**, next door to Wo Fat's, at 111
King Street, is a dim sum dream. **Yung's Kitchen** at 1170
Nuuanu Avenue is practically next door to Pegge
Hopper's gallery. It serves some of Hawaii's best Chinese
dishes in a no-frills dining room, which closes at 11:30
p.m. **Won Kee Seafood Restaurant**, Chinese Cultural
Plaza, 100 N. Beretania Street, will stretch your budget a
bit with every imaginable seafood dish—fried, steamed,
baked, marinated, or otherwise Won Kee'd—but the
result is one of the very best in the state. **Kyoya
Restaurant**, 2057 Kalakaua Avenue, 947-3911, combines
gracious friendliness, atmosphere, excellent food, and
moderate prices. **Food Courts** at Ala Moana's Makai
Market, International Marketplace in Waikiki, and
Windward Mall on Kam Highway in Kaneohe are the best
around for a variety of budget food: Mexican, Hawaiian,
Korean, Chinese, Japanese, Thai, Italian, and American.
Most meals are under $5 and filling.

Where to Stay
North Shore: Haleiwa has no hotels. For a base in
Haleiwa, Alice Tracy's 12 cottages, **Ke Iki Hale** (59-579
Ke Iki Road, Haleiwa, HI 96712, 638-8229), are outstanding but expensive. **Ke Iki Beach** is edged with coconut
palms and ironwoods. At the front door of modest one-
and two-bedroom cottages on the beach and duplex
one-bedrooms behind them, white sand and calm swimming waters prevail in summer and high surf crashes on
rocks in winter. Units cost from $105 to $135 for a one-
bedroom with or without beachfront. The best deal is on
weekly rates. In Mokoleia, condos like the **Mokoleia
Beach Colony** (68-615 Farrington Highway, Waialua, HI
96791, 637-9311) offer very nice units facing the ocean
with minimum stays of a week and $600 weekly mini-
mums, which is still a bargain compared to hotel rates.

Itinerary Options
The **USS *Arizona* Memorial** in Pearl Harbor is in a
very special category as a sightseeing attraction. The
hull of the USS *Arizona* is the tomb of 1,102 men who
died in Japan's surprise attack on December 7, 1941.
The shrine can be visited in two ways: on an excursion
boat, which can't land at the memorial, and by land,
which can be crowded but more informative. Catch a #4
shuttle bus from Waikiki, 926-4747, or TheBus 50 directly to the site where a free shuttle boat ferries you out to
the *Arizona* Memorial. Or drive from Waikiki's
Kalakaua Avenue to Ala Moana Boulevard to Nimitz
Highway (West 92) to H1 West to Highway 90 to USS
Arizona Memorial Visitor Center. From the **Visitor
Center** housing the museum and theater, free navy
shuttle boats run across the harbor (7:45 a.m.-3:00 p.m.)
to a concrete memorial built in 1962 above the aquatic
graveyard. Next to the Memorial Visitor Center, the
Pacific Submarine Museum and its *Bowfin* submarine
are a memorial to 52 submarines and the thousands of
men who died in them during World War II. Open 8:00
a.m. to 4:30 p.m., admission $7 for adults, $1.50 for children age 6 to 12.

Waianae Coast: From 1895 to 1947, the now defunct Oahu Railroad passed through hot and dusty leeward Oahu, along the Waianae Mountains, looping around **Kaena Point**. Today Farrington Highway runs from Honolulu to Kahe Point, passing few restaurants, shops, or hostelries. Most residents are locals. On Kaena Point, according to legend, souls await assignment to heaven or hell, finally exiting from Ghosts' Leap among the black lava rocks.

A safe beach and anchorage, **Pokai Bay Beach Park** backed by mountains is a pretty place for a picnic lunch.

Makaha Beach is famous for its surfing competitions. Follow Makaha Valley Road inland to the **Sheraton Makaha Resort** (P.O. Box 896, Makaha, HI 96792, 800-325-3535 or 695-9511). The Sheraton's 800 renovated bungalows and Polynesian-style buildings sit in an oasis of bougainvillea, hibiscus, and plumeria. Off-season rates of $90 a day double with a car are still possible.

The **Kaala Room** serves elegant dinners in a somewhat formal atmosphere. The view down the valley to the ocean, especially at a legendary Waianae sunset, is one of the most unforgettable parts of the Makaha experience.

The highway continues to **Yokohama Bay** where the pavement end. From here you have to walk to **Kaena Point**. The long stretch of beach along Yokohama Bay is ideal for unofficial camping, especially on **Makua Beach**, the beginning of **Kaena Point State Park**.

DAY 4
MAUI: EXPLORING THE NORTHWEST COAST

After an early morning departure from Honolulu, head directly from Maui's airport to Lahaina for a full morning of sightseeing. After lunch at one of Lahaina's waterfront restaurants, drive north along coastal Highway 30 to Kapalua. Drive up to Pineapple Hill for refreshments on the patio while watching the sunset against a panoramic ocean view. Drive back to Lahaina to get ready for dinner and a night out in Lahaina or, if you plan to see the sunrise from Haleakala's summit, head for bed right after dinner so that you can leave Lahaina tomorrow by 3:00 a.m.

Suggested Schedule

6:00 a.m.	Snack breakfast, check out of hotel, and head for the airport.
7:30 a.m.	Fly from Honolulu to Kahului Airport, Maui.
8:03 a.m.	Arrive in Maui and rent car (or take Gray Line Maui's shuttle from the airport to Lahaina) and check in.
9:15 a.m.	Breakfast in Lahaina.
9:45 a.m.	Walking tour of Lahaina harbor and town.
1:00 p.m.	Lunch on Front Street in Lahaina.
2:00 p.m.	Drive up the coast to Kapalua.
2:30 p.m.	Afternoon swimming and snorkeling at Kapalua Beach.
5:00 p.m.	Refreshments on the patio at Pineapple Hill, Kapalua Resort.
7:30 p.m.	Dinner in Lahaina.
9:00 p.m.	Lahaina or Kaanapali Resort nightlife, or early to bed and early to rise for a sunrise trip to Haleakala.

Getting to Maui

The recently built Kahului Airport receives flights from Aloha Airlines, Hawaiian Air, Aloha Interisland Air, American, Delta, and United.

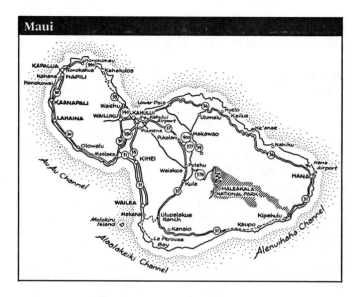

Transportation

There's no public bus system on Maui, so you'll need a car to get around. Reserve one in advance. Ask whether the company has a pickup service at the airport. You'll find an abundance of local car rental companies, more than on any other island, with cars for $25 to $35 per day, flat rate with unlimited mileage. Rent a car right at the airport or get a free ride to car rental offices nearby. In the airport are Alamo Rent-A-Car, 877-3466; American International Rent-A-Car, 877-7604; Andres Rent-A-Car, 877-5378; Avis Rent-A-Car, 877-5167; Budget Rent-A-Car, 871-8811; Dollar Rent-A-Car, 871-8811; Hertz Rent-A-Car, 877-5167; Pacific Rent-A-Car, 877-3065; Robert's Rent-A-Car, 871-6226; and Trans-Maui Rent-A-Car, 877-5222. Outside the airport, older model used cars can be rented at Rent-A-Wreck, 800-367-5230; Uptown Service, 244-0869; and Word of Mouth Rent-A-Used-Car, 877-2436. Other car rental companies include Kamaaina, 877-5460; Maui Car Rental and Leasing, 877-2081; National Car Rental, 877-5347; Sunshine Rent-A-Car, 871-6222; Thrifty Car Rental, 871-7596; and Tropical Rent-A-Car, 877-0002.

Grayline, 877-5507, has a shuttle service from Kahului to Lahaina-Kaanapali for about $11 per person, Trans-

Hawaiian Services, 877-7308, provides a shuttle service
that stops running at 5:00 p.m.

Sightseeing Highlights
▲▲▲**Lahaina**—This was the political center of the
Hawaiian kingdom from about 1800 to 1945. Around
1820, the town became the main provisioning stop for
whaling ships and the playground for thousands of seamen and quickly lost its innocence. About the same time,
missionaries arrived for a classic confrontation between
salvation and sin. In 1962, Lahaina was designated a
National Historic Landmark. In the same year, the
Lahaina Restoration Foundation was formed to restore
the historic sites along Front Street. The rapidly growing
collection of shops, galleries, restaurants, and other
attractions draws millions of visitors annually and produces traffic jams and parking problems. Lahaina now
stretches 2 miles, four blocks deep. The heart of the
town is a one-third-mile stretch between Shaw and
Papalaua streets. Front Street, the main shopping and
entertainment strip, runs between these streets.

The Cannery, a large air-conditioned shopping mall
opened in 1987 in a former pineapple cannery and located on Highway 30 as you leave Lahaina, recently was
joined by another 150,000 square feet of shopping mall
extending between Front Street and Highway 30.
Altogether, Lahaina shopping space far exceeds Ala
Moana on Oahu and is approaching Waikiki. Where or
when will it stop? Be sure to stop at the Lahaina Print-
sellers on Front Street in the historic Seamen's Hospital
and the Village Gallery (the Cannery and 120 Dickenson
Street, Lahaina; the Embassy Suites, Kaanapali).

The historic places to see are within a few blocks of
Front Street. The banyan tree, planted behind the court-
house on April 24, 1873, by Sheriff William Owen Smith
to commemorate the 50th anniversary of Lahaina's first
Protestant mission, is the largest in the islands, covering
about two-thirds of an acre. On the harbor side of the
banyan tree are the coral stone ruins of the Old Fort con-
structed in the 1830s to protect missionaries' homes from

whalers. The Pioneer Inn, built in 1901, had the only accommodations in west Maui until the late 1950s. Across Papelekane Street is the Brick Palace, the first Western-style building in the islands, built by Kamehameha I. Across from the Pioneer Inn on Front Street is the Baldwin Home Museum, the New England-style residence with furnishings of medical missionary Dwight Baldwin, whose offspring became some of the largest landowners in the islands.

Carthaginian II, anchored in the harbor directly opposite the Pioneer Inn, is a two-masted square-rigged replica of the ship that went aground in 1920. It contains a museum exhibit of the whaling era. Open from 9:00 a.m. to 4:30 p.m. Admission is $3 for adults; accompanied children are admitted free.

Waiola Church, the first stone church in the islands (circa 1830), has been rebuilt several times, the latest in 1953, when the name was changed from "Wainee" in an attempt to change its luck. Waiola Cemetery behind the church dates back to 1823. Many Hawaiian chiefs and queens who became Christians are buried there.

Wo Hing Society Hall on Front Street, built in 1912 by Chinese laborers imported to the island, has a small museum and social hall. Lahaina Jodo Mission at 12 Ala Moana Street, founded in 1921, contains the 12-foot bronze and copper giant Buddha cast in Japan and sent to Maui in 1968 for a centennial celebration of the first Japanese immigrants to Hawaii.

▲▲**Kaanapali Resort**—Starting four miles north of Lahaina, this is the beginning of the west Maui Gold Coast that continues ten miles to Kapalua. The 500-acre resort contains seven hotels, including the new Embassy Suites, five condominium complexes, two golf courses, a shopping center, and miles of sandy beaches. Beyond Kaanapali are the condominium "villages" of Honokowai, Kahana, Napili, and Kapalua. Highway 30 (the Hono a Piilani Highway) circles west Maui.

Visit the Whalers Village Museum on the third floor of Whalers Village Shopping Center (9:30 a.m. to 9:30 p.m., closed 1:00 to 1:30 p.m.) to see a unique display of whal-

ing artifacts and photos and a 30-minute whale video
shown every half hour.

The best place to swim and snorkel in the Kaanapali
Resort is next to Black Rock (Pu'u Keka'a) at the
Sheraton Hotel's beach. The great mid-eighteenth-century
king-warrior, Kahikili, leaped from this ancient "leaping
place" of souls into their ancestral spiritland. This event is
reenacted nightly by divers from the hotel.

▲**"Sugar Cane Train" (Lahaina-Kaanapali & Pacific
Railroad)**—An oil-fired narrow gauge steam locomotive
(Anaka or Myrtle), refurbished to resemble a vintage
sugarcane locomotive, carries you in an open passenger
car on a six-mile excursion past golf courses, cane fields,
and ocean views. The train makes five 25-minute (one-
way) trips daily between the Puukolii Boarding Platform
(across from the Royal Lahaina) and the Lahaina Station,
with a stop at the Kaanapali Station. A one-way ticket is
$7.50, round-trip $11.

Where to Stay

If you have a car, anywhere in the Lahaina, Kaanapali,
Honokowai, and Napili Bay area can serve as a base for
the day or the entire stay on Maui. The highest-priced
accommodations are in Wailea, Kaanapali, and Kapalua;
next is Kahana, with a resort atmosphere and mostly high-
rise condos. Kihei and Honokowai's mix of older and
newer, high- and low-rise condos are the largest "moderate" priced collection of vacation units on the island.

In Lahaina, the **Plantation Inn** is a Victorian-style hotel
near the waterfront, with 9 units ($99-$145 with breakfast,
174 Lahuainaluna Road, Lahaina, Maui HI 96761, 800-433-
6815, 667-9225). The inn is one of a kind and right near
the heart of town. **Gerard's** restaurant occupies the front
of the building and guests receive a 20 to 40 percent discount on dinners, which offsets the high room cost.

Lahaina Hotel, Lahaina, a 13-room inn with turn-of-the-
century charm and every modern convenience, is decorated with the utmost taste (127 Lahainaluna Rd., Lahaina,
Maui 96761, 800-669-3444 or 661-0577). Rates are $89 to
$99 standard single or double, including breakfast.

Lahaina Shores Beach Resort was re-created from the ground up, and the Victorian architecture seems to fit old Lahaina ($115-$175, 475 Front Street, Lahaina, Maui, HI 96761, 800-628-6699 or 661-4835).

Kaanapali Alii, Kaanapali, is sited on beautiful grounds next to the beach ($175-$250, 50 Nohea Kai Drive, Kaanapali, Maui HI 96761, 800-642-MAUI or 667-1400). A one-bedroom garden unit ($80) at the **Maui Sands**, 3559 Lower Hono a Piilani, Lahaina, 96761, 669-9110 (or 800-367-5037), is one of the best budget accommodations in Honokowai. You pay more for newer oceanside units, more luxurious furnishings, and lanais with views. The older **Honokowai Palms**, 3666 Lower Hono a Piilani Highway, Lahaina 96761, 667-2712 or toll-free 800-669-MAUI, is across the street from the beach with one-bedroom oceanview units, or two-bedroom apartments without ocean view, for two at $75. **Paki Maui**, Honokawi, on the beach, has charming rooms, lush landscaping of the grounds, lanais for outstanding views of Molokai ($119-$170, Aston Hotels & Resorts, 2255 Kuhio, Honolulu, HI 96815, 800-535-0085 or 669-8325).

The best value for the money in the Napili area is the **Coconut Inn**, 181 Hui Road, Napili, 96761, 800-367-8006 or 669-5712. Forty-one units on two levels are tucked in a lovely garden setting (with pool and hot tub) away from the main road on a hill overlooking Napili. Comfortable studio units for two with kitchen and tub/shower cost $85 including a delicious continental breakfast. Also try **Napili Sunset**, 46 Hui Road (669-8083, 800-447-9229), right on Napili Bay if their 88 units are available, $85 garden studio. **Napili Point** (115 rooms) is located next to the second-best beach on West Maui, with panoramic views from its lanais (5295 Honoapilani Highway, Napili, Maui HI 96761, 800-922-7866 or 669-9222), $85 studio with garden view.

Kapalua Bay, Kapalua, contains only 200 units of stylish luxury (reminiscent of the Big Island's Mauna Kea) in three-story buildings open to beautifully land-scaped rolling hills to the ocean and one of the most perfect crescent beaches on Maui ($220-$400, 1 Bay Drive, Kapalua, Maui HI 96761, 800-367-8000 or 669-5656). **Kapalua Villas** has luxurious rooms with wonderful views of the Pacific spread out over green sloping acreage to 3 beaches and several golf courses ($155-$390, 1 Bay Drive, Kapalua, Maui HI 96761, 800-367-8000 or 669-5656).

Cabins: The cabins at state parks and private cabins in Hana are the most economical and enjoyable way for adventuresome people to spend a vacation on Maui with a base either in Hana or on Haleakala. The same is true for official camping sites located in roughly the same areas. **Hana Bay Vacation Rentals**, the best way to find cabins in Hana, some in secluded settings, also has apartments and homes ranging from $70 to $250, 800-657-7970 or 248-7726. **Waianapanapa State Park** has housekeeping cabins, $10 per person per night. **Polipoli Springs State Park** offers a single cabin for $10 single, $14 double. **Haleakala National Park** has three multibunk cabins (Kaalaoa, Paliku, and Hokua Cabins) on the crater floor assigned by lottery.

Official Camping: Waianapanapa State Park on the outskirts of Hana; Kaumahina State Wayside Park en route to Hana; Oheo Gulch on the bluffs over the sea; Poli Poli State Park.

Unofficial Camping: Oneloa Beach Park and Honolua Bay north of Kapalua; Poolenalena Beach Park, nearby Black Sands Beach and Makena Beach (all just a few miles from the Wailea Shopping Center).

Where to Eat

Avalon Restaurant, in the courtyard of Mariners Alley (844 Front Street, 667-5559), is one of the two best new East-meets-West restaurants in Maui and Hawaii. **David Paul's Lahaina Grill** (127 Lahainaluna Road, 667-5117) is the second. It takes eclectic flavors and cooking styles and applies them to fresh local produce. Go to the **Bay Club** (669-5656, Kapalua Bay Hotel) for nouvelle cuisine by candlelight. **Haliimaile General Store** (900 Haiimaile Road, 572-2666), a plantation store converted into a gourmet dining treat, is off the beaten track. **Hana-Maui** (Hotel Hana-Maui, 248-8211) serves expensive prix fixe dining in a beautiful setting. **La Bretagne** (661-8966) has fine french food in elegant yet comfortable surroundings. **Mama's Fish House** (between Paia and Hookipa Beach Park, 579-8030) serves delicious fish, is more expensive than you think, of course, and is worth it. **The Bakery** (next to the LKRR depot, 667-9062, 991 Limahina Place) sells croissant, brioche, and other baked goods that rival Jacques on Kauai, which says a lot, and any bake shop in Hawaii. **The Prince Court** (Maui Prince, Makena, 874-1111) prepares American cuisine with a fresh creative touch in every dish. **Raffles** (Stouffer Wailea Resort, 879-4900) does indeed live up to its awards and reputation (despite some rumors to the contrary). **Saeng's Thai Cuisine** (2119 Vineyard Street, 244-1568) or **Siam Thai** (123 N. Market Street, 244-3817) in Wailuku are a toss-up for the best Thai food on Maui. **Swan Court** (Hyatt regency Maui, Kaanapali, 661-1234) is an ultra-elegant and romantic splurge.

On the way through Kihei, stop at **Paradise Fruit Stand** (1913 S. Kihei Rd., in Kihei) for fresh fruit and especially smoothies.

Try a breakfast of the best coconut, banana, or macadamia nut pancakes or a lunch of seafood chowder on the terrace of the Pioneer Inn's **Harpooner's Lanai**, 658 Wharf Street. On the Kaanapali side of Lahaina, **Lahaina Natural Foods**, 1295 Front Street, has fresh baked goods, a very good deli, and great sandwiches to take out. Take out an Italian picnic lunch for the beach from **Longhi's Pizzeria Deli**, 930 Wainee Street.

A gourmet splurge dinner or lunch in the courtyard of charming **Gerard's**, located in the extraordinary Plantation Inn, 174 Lahainaluna Road (661-8939), is one of the outstanding dining experiences in Hawaii. Chef Gerard Reversade creatively changes his menus daily, and all of the beef, veal, duck, chicken, seafood, and other surprises are superbly prepared with the freshest ingredients and elegant sauces. Five miles south of Lahaina, about a ten-minute scenic drive, **Chez Paul**,

820-B Olowalu Village, 661-3843, has two seatings (6:30 p.m. and 8:30 p.m.) for excellent French cuisine. **Ricco's**, 661-4433, in the Whaler's Village complex, offers buffet platters and a variety of excellent subs that qualify as family budget meals.

Plan a predinner drink watching the sun sink over Molokai from the renowned patio of the **Plantation House Restaurant**, Plantation Golf Course Club House, 2000 Plantation Club Dr., 669-6129, set high above Kapalua's beachfront resort. Surprisingly, some of the best dinner values can be found at dinner buffets at the big resorts, especially during summer months. Check out the seafood or regular buffet at the **Westin Maui** and the **Marriott's Moano Terrace** next door at Kaanapali.

Nightlife

The **Old Lahaina Luau**, the best luau on Maui, provides authentic Hawaiian food on the beach behind Whaler's Marketplace (505 Front Street, 667-1998), Tuesday through Saturday evenings at 5:30 p.m. to catch the sunset, $46 for adults and $23 for children 12 and under. See the hula show at the **Kaanapali Beach Hotel's Tiki Terrace** nightly from 6:30 to 7:30 p.m.

Upcountry has only one nightlife spot worth mentioning, and only on weekends—the **Casanova Restaurant** in the center of Makawao. **The Old Whaler's Grog Shop** in the Pioneer Inn and the **Whale's Tale Restaurant** on Front Street are for drinking and fun. **Jazz at Blackie's Bar** (667-7979) is another local and tourist favorite just outside of Lahaina on the Kaanapali side.

On Friday evenings, **"Art Night in Lahaina,"** from 7:00 to 9:00 p.m., galleries present artists, free entertainment, and refreshments. Strolling around Lahaina and people-watching between shopping, eating, and pub-crawling is entertainment enough. In addition, Lahaina's bars around Front Street and in the shopping complexes have all the music and activity you want. The **Lahaina Broiler** hops until midnight. Disco at **Moose McGillicuddy's** nightly. On weekends, it's Hawaiian music at the **Banyan Inn** and dancing at **Longhi's** on Friday and Saturday nights. The $22 luau and cocktail or $36 dinner show ("Drums of the Pacific") at **Hyatt Regency** is one of the best in Kaanapali. Disco at the Hyatt's **Spats II** is one of the most popular on the island (open to 4:00 a.m.). Before or after, you can walk around the hotel's public areas to window-shop and view the displays of Oriental art. The disco at the Maui Marriott, the **Banana Moon**, is open until 1:30 a.m. and may be to your liking.

Itinerary Options
Molokini Island: According to Hawaiian legend, Pele's dream-lover, Lohi-au, married a *mo'o* (dragon), incurring Pele's terrible wrath. The volatile fire goddess swiftly cut the mo'o in half: one-half became Puu Olai hill in Makena, and the other half became known as Molokini. Five azure blue miles from the white sands of Wailea and Makena, crescent-shaped Molokini Island surrounds the largest concentration of tropical fish in all of Hawaii. The 150-foot volcanic tuff cone (Maui's only one) opens to the north with a protective semicircle embracing more than 200 species of fish, many varieties of seaweed, reef coral, and a vast array of other sea creatures unwittingly enjoying the protections of Molokini Shoal Marine Life Conservation District.

Only accessible by boat, Molokini can be reached in 20 minutes on the *Kai Kanani* (879-7218), a sleek 46-foot sailing catamaran that departs from Makena. Arrangements for this wonderful morning snorkeling can be made at the Maui Prince/Ocean Activities desk (879-4485). Continental breakfast comes with the cruise and all snorkel gear, lunch, and sodas ($45). Nonsnorkelers instead can arrange for a champagne sunset dinner sail that leaves from **Maalaea Harbor** on Monday, Wednesday, and Friday (879-4485). Sail at 7:30 a.m. or noon on the 60-foot *Lavengro* out of Maalaea Harbor for Molokini Crater, with continental breakfast and a buffet lunch or on the *Trilogy* for a half-day excursion from Maalaea Harbor.

Lahaina is a center for water sports activities—cruises, sailing, snorkeling, scuba diving, fishing, and whale-watching. Arrange for any of these activities at the Lahaina Beach Center, 661-5959, or the Lahaina Sea Sport Center, 667-2759. For about $45, you can take either the *Kaulana,* a 70-foot motor-powered catamaran, 667-2518, or the three-masted schooner *Spirit of Windjammer,* Windjammer Cruises, 667-6834 or 800-843-8113, with dinner and open bar.

Deep-sea fishing runs about $65 a half day on a share basis and $125 to $150 for an eight-hour day at Aerial Sportfishing, 667-9089; Lahaina Charter Boats, 667-6672; and Aloha Activity Center, 667-9564. Whale-watching excursions from January through April leave Lahaina Harbor in the morning and afternoon and cost $25 for an adult. Contact Seabird Cruises, 661-3643, or Windjammer Cruises, or book a cruise through the Pacific Whale Foundation, 879-6530. The price is $27.50 for adults, $15 for children 3 to 12. Check the Whale Report Center, 661-8527, for the latest report on whale sightings.

Snorkel at the Sheraton, next to Black Rock. Park at the Whaler's Shopping Center to walk to the beach. (The Sheraton parking lot actually has a few spaces reserved for beach users.) Better still, drive out Highway 30 to Honolua Bay (except in winter), walk a few hundred yards, and try the best snorkeling on Maui. Otherwise, half-day excursions, with lunch or breakfast, to Molokai and Lanai or just offshore cost from $80 to $110 through American Dive of Maui, 661-4885; Central Pacific Divers, 661-8718 or 800-551-6767; Dive Maui, 667-2080; Hawaiian Reef Divers, 667-7647; Lahaina Divers, 667-7496; and Scuba Schools of Maui, 661-8036. Snorkelers, contact Maui Adventures, 661-3400, or Snorkeling Hawaii, 661-8156, for two-hour cruises out of Lahaina at about $25 per person.

Surfing is best in the summer at Lahaina and Kaanapali. Check with Lahaina Dive & Surf, 667-6001. Otherwise, for experienced surfers, Honolua Bay and Hookipa Beach Park on the North Shore and Hamoa Beach in Hana are the best spots on Maui.

If you have extra time, drive around the **West Maui Mountains**. Make sure you have a full gas tank. Four of Maui's prettiest beaches are located on this route, all off Route 30 north of Kapalua, each with different onshore scenery and sense of seclusion; three of them are bounded by cliffs: **D. T. Fleming Park**, under palm or ironwood trees, with a view of Molokai; **Oneloa Beach**, past D. T. Fleming Park, white sand in a cove backed by cliffs, with good swimming and snorkeling; **Honolua Bay**, near Oneloa Beach, under lovely trees near the water; and **Pohakupule** or **Windmill Beach**, a white sand beach surrounded by cliffs. Farther north, neat **Kahakuloa**, the Kahakuloa Valley Trail passes through one of Maui's untouched areas.

Driving from Kapalua to Wailuku takes about three hours. Route 330 changes to Route 340 at Honokohau Bay and becomes a rutted dirt road that your car rental agency hates; they will not accept responsibility for car damage. (Check first to see if the road is passable or washed out, which happens. Actually, you're following an old royal horse trail.) Pass picturesque **Kahakuloa**, cliffs, valleys, and lush fern gulches between razorbacked ridges that run from Puu Kukui's mile-high summit to the sea. After the road becomes paved again in the cane plantation town of Waihee, a side road leads up to **Halekii Heiau**, once football field-size temples, now rubble.

Helicopter tours are very expensive and thrilling. If you can spend $100 to $300 (depending on the season) to see west Maui, Haleakala, Hana, the whole island, or Molokai, it's well worth it. Flightseeing excursions with Papillon Helicopters, 800-367-7095 or 669-4884, depart from the Pineapple Hill Helipad near Kapalua, fly over the West Maui Mountains, and land in a wilderness spot for a champagne picnic. Papillon also has a flight that will get you to Haleakala for sunrise, followed by a visit to Hana.

MAUI: HALEAKALA VOLCANO AND UPCOUNTRY

Haleakala (House of the Sun), the world's largest dormant volcano, a "Mt. Everest" in the Pacific, rises from 20,000 feet under the sea to over 10,000 feet above sea level. As the sun rises or sets, its light paints pastel streaks on the massed clouds and edges the crater's vast rim in red and golden hues. Only high priests and sorcerers dared to reside in this spellbinding place. Today, 63 miles from Lahaina, you visit the summit of Haleakala National Park, preferably at sunrise, and hike some of the crater's shorter trails before descending to the volcano's lower slopes—Upcountry.

Suggested Schedule

3:00 a.m.	Phone for weather report: 572-7749. Then head east on Highway 378 to Haleakala. (Too early? Then leave at 6:00 and arrive at the summit way too late for sunrise.)
5:30 a.m.	Park Headquarters and then Puu Ulaula Visitor's Center at Haleakala summit for sunrise or early morning views.
6:30 a.m.	Snack breakfast at summit before venturing out on the crater trails.
7:00 a.m.	Walk on Halemauu or Sliding Sands Trail.
10:00 a.m.	Return to Visitor's Center to see exhibits and hear talk by ranger.
12:00 noon	Descend for lunch in Upcountry.
2:00 p.m.	Browsing and shopping in Makawao and Paia.
3:30 p.m.	Kula Botanical Gardens.
4:30 p.m.	Tedeschi Winery for wine-tasting.
6:00 p.m.	Sunset from Kula (or as an option, on Haleakala).
7:00 p.m.	Dinner in Makawao and overnight in Upcounty.

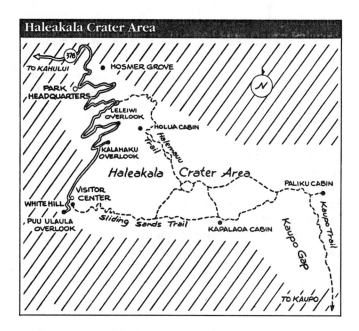

Haleakala Crater Area

Sightseeing Highlights

▲▲▲**Haleakala**—This eerie pyramid of incredibly dense volcanic rock has a 3,000-foot-deep crater dwarfing nine cinder cone mountains across its floor, including thousand-foot-high Puu O Maui. Frequently, misty clouds surround the 7-mile-long, 2-mile-wide crater, obscuring its 21 miles of rim from view. Before starting the 2-hour drive from Lahaina (1 hour from Kahului) to the summit of Haleakala, phone for a taped report on weather and travel conditions. Start early because clouds begin rolling in by 9:00 or 10:00 a.m. *Dress warmly* (sweaters or parka), especially for sunrise and sunset excursions. Prepare to freeze and fry. Bring insulated clothing, a blanket and mittens, rain gear and sun protection, including hats and sunscreen, lunch and plenty of liquids, as well as cameras, plenty of film, and binoculars.

From Kahului, go southeast on Highway 37 about 10 miles to Pukalani, then turn east (left) on Highway 377. After 6 miles of climbing through cane and then pineapple fields, turn east again onto Highway 378, which snakes 12 miles to Park Headquarters through pastures and rocky wastelands at higher elevations. It's over 10 miles from Park Headquarters to the summit. Drive carefully on the many switchbacks.

At Halemauu Trail (8,000 feet), walk a mile to the crater rim, where you can see the trail zigzagging down the crater wall, or wait until you reach the Leleiwi Overlook for the same view closer to the road. At Kalahaku Overlook you'll see silverswords, the Hawaii state flower that takes 4 to 20 years to bloom once (sometime from May through October) and then dies.

Two visitor's shelters await at the summit: the Haleakala Visitor's Center on the rim has exhibits and hourly talks explaining the region's geology and legends; and the glass-enclosed Puu Ulaula Visitor's Center on the summit (Red Hill), where you see the unforgettable sunrises or sunsets, is an easy quarter-mile hike past stone shelters and sleeping platforms used by Hawaiians who came up to quarry iron-hard stone for tools.

After spending all the time you want on the summit, go down inside the crater. Sliding Sands, the main crater trail, starts near the Visitor's Center. (You can return to the road via Halemauu Trail, hitching back to the summit.) As you descend Sliding Sands Trail, through cinders and ash, you can see the contrasting lush forests of the Koolau Gap. It's about four miles to the crater floor. On the drive down, stop a mile past the park entrance at Hosmer Grove (7,030 feet) for a walk on the nature trail through cedar, spruce, juniper, pines, and trees imported from Australia, India, and Japan.

▲▲▲**Upcountry**—This area encircles Haleakala from Haiku and the cowboy town of Makawao to Kula, Poli Poli State Park above Kula, and out Highway 37 to the Ulupalakua Ranch and the Tedeschi Winery, part of the 37,000-acre ranch. The rich volcanic soil of Kula makes it Maui's flower and vegetable garden spot. Just before Route 37 joins Route 377, native koas, kukul trees, Norfolk Island pine, bamboo orchids, proteas, and native and imported flora grow in the Kula Botanical Gardens. This is a perfect spot for a picnic lunch. The gardens display more than 700 types of plants, open 9:00 a.m. to 4:00 p.m., adults $2.50, 878-1715.

To visit the Tedeschi Winery, 878-6058, turn left on Highway 370 through the town of Keokea (take the right-hand fork in the road, which has no sign) and pass the Ulupalakua Ranch. Allow at least half an hour before 5:00 p.m. closing time. On the way back to Kahului, turn right in Pukalani on Highway 365 for Makawao (or, if it's too late, save Makawao for Day 7 on the way back from Hana, taking the back way through Ulumalu). In Makawao, the unofficial capital of Upcountry, behind Old West wooden storefronts you'll find espresso, bagels and cream cheese, more and more boutiques, and galleries favoring local artists down Baldwin Avenue. Farther down Baldwin Avenue is the Hai Noeau Visual Arts Center on the lovely Baldwin estate.

Where to Stay

Kula and Olinda: Upcountry is a cool, lush, laid-back mountain retreat. The B&Bs in Kula and nearby Olinda reinforce this get-away-from-it-all experience

Jody Baldwin's **Kilohana B&B** (378 Kamehameki Rd., Kula, HI 96790, 878-6086, $60-$80) is in a perfect location for driving up Haleakala at sunrise or anytime. From the 3,600-foot level of Kula's slopes, the porch and spacious garden offer panoramic views. Jody herself is one of the most hospitable, delightful, and informed B&B proprietors in Hawaii.

Another outstanding Upcountry B&B, with marvelous views and surroundings, is Stewart and Shaun **McKay's Country Cottage B&B** (536 Olinda Rd., Makawao, Maui, HI 96768, 572-1453). At the top of Olinda Road, 4,000 feet up the slopes of Haleakala, the McKay's "manor house" sits in the midst of a 12-acre protea flower farm. Located five miles above Makawao, beautiful, winding Olinda Road is one of the loveliest drives in Hawaii. The lovely McKay cottage sleeps four and rents for $95 for two and $18 each additional person with breakfast.

In the midst of a pineapple farm, the **Gildersleeve's B&B** (2112 Naalae Road, Kula, Maui, HI 96790, 878-6623, $50-$85) has three attractively furnished guest bedrooms with private baths in the main house and a cottage.

Kihei: While Wailea and Makena were evolving as planned developments, condominiums were springing up like weeds west of Wailea along the Kihei Coast. Maalaea/Kihei became a six-mile stretch of increasingly haphazard development, mostly high- and low-rise condos, cottage hostelries, and a few hotels, with shopping centers in Kihei every few blocks.

Kihei's advantages over other locations of Maui consists of a combination of less expensive accommodations, ample sunshine, and easy access to some very good beaches in Kihei and in Wailea and Makena.

The price certainly is right for accommodations in Kihei ($80-$160). Moderately priced condominiums are plentiful. Some of the beaches and beachfront parks are among the most attractive on Maui and in Hawaii, usually no farther than across the road from these accommodations. These hotel/condominiums are standouts at rates ranging from $80 to $105 in season and less off-season: **Maui Sunset** (1032 S. Kihei Rd., Kihei, Maui HI 96753, 800-843-5880 or 879-0674), **Hale Kamaole** (2737 S. Kihei Rd., Kihei, Maui HI 96753, 800-367-2970 or 879-2698), **Koa Resort** (811 S. Kihei Rd., Kihei, Maui 96753, 800-877-1314 or 879-1161), **Maui Lu Resort** (575 S. Kihei Rd., Kihei, Maui HI 96753, 800-922-7866), and **Nani Kai Hale** (73 N. Kihei Rd., Kihei, Maui 96753, 800-367-6032 or 879-9120). Some of these condominiums, like Nani Kai Hale, have minimum stay requirements of seven days in season. Ask about off-season discounts, rental car and airport pickup packages, and air-conditioning if it's important to you.

Additional moderate-priced ($70-$90 for one-bedroom apartments for two persons in season) choices of condo/hotel accommodations, either on the beach or across from it, include **Kamaole Beach Royale Resort** (2385 S. Kihei Rd., Kihei, Maui, HI 96753, 879-3131 or toll-free 800-421-3661), **Kihei Kai** (61 N. Kihei Rd., Kihei, Maui, HI 96753, 879-2357 or toll-free 800-735-2357), **Mana-Kai Maui Condominium Hotel** (2960 S. Kihei Rd., Kihei, Maui, HI 96753, 879-1561 or toll-free 800-525-2025), and the **Sunseeker Resort** (551 S. Kihei Rd., Kihei, Maui, HI 96753, 879-1261).

In a category by themselves are Dave Kong's eight
Nona Lani Cottages ($70-$85, 455 S Kihei Rd. Kihei,
Maui HI 96753, 879-2497 or toll-free 800-733-2688), set
back from the road in a landscaped setting, and the least
expensive cottages in Kihei, Tad and Kimberley Fuller's
Lihi Kai Cottages (2121 Iliili Rd., Kihei, Maui HI 96753,
800-LIHIKAI OR 879-2335), in an excellent location
(except for traffic noise in some units) near Kalama Park.
Nearby shopping at the Kamaole Shopping Center,
Dolphin Shopping Center, Azeka's Place Shopping
Center, and numerous other stores make this one of the
most convenient and economical places to spend a few
days.

Where to Eat
A big, sophisticated Italian eating surprise in Makawao is
Casanova's, 1188 Makawao Ave., 572-0220, $10 to $14 à
la carte, delicious food. **Polli's Cantina**, 1202 Makawao
Ave., 572-7808, is an excellent vegetarian Mexican restaurant with full dinners for $8 to $12. Until you get to Lihue
on Kauai, you won't find better or less expensive saimin
than at **Kitada's**, 572-7241, on Baldwin Avenue across
from the **Makawao Steak House**, 572-8711. At 89 Hana
Highway in Paia, **Dillon's Restaurant**, 579-9113, is a
home away from home for hungry travelers with a taste
for artistic cooking and drinks. Stop for breakfast en
route to Hana. **Mama's Fish House**, 579-9672, right on
the beach in Kuau Cove about 1 mile outside of Paia,
serves fresh ono with Hana ginger and Maui onions, a
perfect house salad, chilled papaya coconut soup,
Mama's homemade bread, and luscious desserts, moderately expensive but worth it.

In Wailuku, across from the Happy Valley Inn, at 309
N. Market Street, **Yori's** serves Japanese, American, and
especially Hawaiian food. Try squid in coconut milk. For
quick and cheap snacks in Kihei, the top choices are
Suda's Snack Shop, 61 South Kihei Road, and a plate
lunch at **Azeka's Snack Shop**, in Azeka's Place
Shopping Center. For the best bargain breakfast with the
best view of Wailea, have all-you-can-eat pancakes for

$2.95 on the patio of the **Makena Golf Course Restaurant** (879-1154).

For delicious splurge dinners, **Hakone's** Japanese food and environment at the Maui Prince Resort, Makena, are unsurpassed in the islands as is **La Perouse** at the Maui Inter-Continental (879-1922) for continental dining in an Oriental decor.

Itinerary Options

Highway 377 leads to the **Poli Poli Springs Recreation Area** and the **Kula Forest Reserve**. After a rugged but beautiful drive through towering trees on Waipoli Road off Highway 377, definitely requiring a four-wheel-drive vehicle, a four-mile hike leads to spectacular views from the 6,000-foot level on slopes over Ulupalakua. (One of Ken Schmitt's fabulous **Hiking Maui** trips, 879-5270, includes Poli Poli, solving the transportation problem.) If you decide to drive to Poli Poli by yourself, consider staying overnight or for several days at the park's three-bedroom cabin ($10 per night for 1 person, less per person for each additional person), which has to be reserved well in advance with the Division of Parks (54 High Street, Wailuku, HI 96793, 244-4354).

The special experience of Upcountry touring should include a visit to Sunrise Market or another of Kula's small protea or vegetable farms. Kula is famous for its protea, one of the most amazing and beautiful varieties of flowers, with huge blossoms in 1,400 amazing varieties. These botanical wonders are grown by Upcountry farmers like John Hiroshima (**Sunrise Market and Protea Farm**, 878-2119, on Route 378 three miles past the Haleakala National Park turnoff).

If you have good bicycle riding skills, good conditioning, better nerves, and the inclination to bike down from the summit of Haleakala, **Cruiser Bob's Haleakala Downhill**, 667-7717, offers a sunrise trip (3:00 a.m. departure), including continental breakfast and champagne brunch, or an 8:00 a.m. departure with continental breakfast and a picnic lunch halfway down, for about $100 per person.

MAUI: HANA

On your way to the fabled village of Hana through a tunnel of foliage, surprise views open from hairpin turns. One-lane bridges pass over gleaming gulches and reveal sparkling waterfalls flowing from Haleakala, carving valleys for coconut, monkeypod, mango, wild ginger, plumeria, bamboo, breadfruit, koa, and banana trees. Isolated villages appear and then disappear just as quickly. Trails beckon to picnic areas near swimming holes under waterfalls. Hana is a Hawaii unto itself, preserving the beauty and spirit that have attracted ancient Hawaiians and modern celebrities.

Suggested Schedule

7:00 a.m.	Kahului-Wailuku or Kula to Paia for breakfast (last stop for gas and food).
8:00 a.m.	Drive Hana Highway with as many or as few stops as you wish.
11:30 a.m.	Arrive Hana.
12:00 noon	Stroll and/or swim at Hamoa Beach.
1:00 p.m.	Lunch in Hana or picnic at Waianapanapa State Park.
2:00 p.m.	Option: Ohe'o Gulch trip.
2:30 p.m.	Visit Helani Gardens.
4:15 p.m.	Browse in Hasegawa's General Store.
5:15 p.m.	Sunset at Hana Bay or some other view point.
6:30 p.m.	Dinner in Hana and overnight.

Sightseeing Highlights

▲▲▲**The Hana Highway (Route 36)**—Acclaimed as one of the most beautiful drives in Hawaii, paved in 1962, the "highway" still has one-lane bridges and hairpin turns that haven't been straightened a bit. It's only 52 miles, but allow at least 3 hours to zigzag at 10 to 25 miles per hour through the 600 bumpy, twisting turns and over 50 one-lane bridges to Hana. Don't try a round-

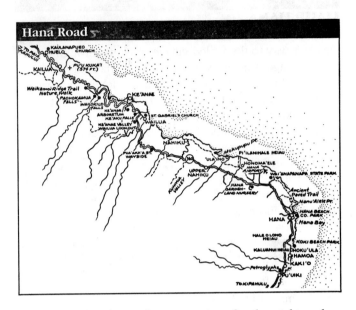

trip in one day, but make reservations for the night and
return via Hana Road tomorrow. Day-trippers outnumber
the local population, so start early to get ahead of the traffic.

Stop for breakfast in quaint and weatherbeaten Paia, a
former sugar town that once had a population of over
10,000. To visit Twin Falls and its idyllic swimming
holes, drive about 15 minutes down the jeep trail to the
double waterfall and first pool, then walk down to the
others.

Pause at **Huelo's** New England-style Kaulanapueo
Church (1853) en route to the turnout for the nature trail
through bamboo and trees on Waikamoi Ridge. Campers
already may have found Kaumahina State Wayside and its
rain forest campground overlooking the sea and another
pool at nearby Puohokamoa Falls. Tucked in the rugged
coastline is the black sand beach at Honomanu Bay.
Keanae Arboretum's tropical gardens cover the spectrum
of Hawaiian plant life: rain forest, plants, flowers, and
vegetables. Circle the peninsula to the dead end for views
of old Hawaii's farms growing taro and a splendid view of
Haleakala.

Other side roads bring you to the fishing village of Wailua and Wailua Lookout, Puaa Kaa State Park, and nearby waterfalls. A few miles away is another picturesque fishing village, Nahiku. The Miracle Church of Wailua on Wailua Road at the 18-mile marker is so named because a storm left Wailua Bay strewn with the coral that enabled parishioners to build the church. Just before the airport and Hana Gardenland Nursery is the turnoff to Piilanihale Heiau, with 50-foot-high walls, reputed to be Hawaii's largest. Stop again at beautiful Waianapanapa State Park's black sand beach on Pailoa Bay, where you can swim and snorkel on a calm day, walk the rocky lava-strewn King's Trail past blowholes and magnificent coastal scenery, and see Waianapanapa Caves, a lava tube. Garden lovers should visit wonderful Helani Gardens, 248-8274, open only 2:00 p.m. to 4:00 p.m., admission $2 for adults, $1 for children 6 to 16, with a tremendous variety of groomed and wild trees and plants.

▲▲▲**Hana**—Hana's main attractions are Red Sand Beach and cove, reached by a tricky footpath from the parking area at the end of Uakea Road, behind the Hana School and Hana Community Center; Waianapanapa State Park's scenic ancient Hawaiian coastal trail to Hana over volcanic rock (requiring very sturdy shoes) which passes within a stone's throw of the park's 12 housekeeping cabins in a forest of *hala* trees; the very scenic, twisting road to Ohe'o Gulch (Seven Sacred Pools) and the hike up the gulch to Makahiku Falls, or especially, for the more physically fit, the 1½ miles through an exotic bamboo forest to Waimoku Falls; Hana Ranch (248-7238) trail rides (breakfast or dinner) along Hana's scenic coastline or to hidden waterfalls or four-wheel-drive ranch safari tours through unspoiled countryside to see their modern ranching system. By arrangement with the Hotel Hana-Maui, visit the otherwise inaccessible fifteenth-century Piilanihale, Hawaii's largest heiau (340 ft. x 415 ft. terraced stone platform). If you're a guest of the Hana-Maui, ask them to pack a picnic lunch for excursions to any of these locations.

The Hana Cultural Center (*Hale O Waiwai 'O Hana* or Hana's House of Treasures) on Uakea Road, a one-room wooden building, displays artifacts from the area and handicrafts of local residents (10:30 a.m. to 5:00 p.m. Mon.-Sat., 10:00 a.m.-noon on Sunday, 248-8622). At the end of Uakea Road starts the path to beautiful and secluded Red Sand Beach.

The cluttered Hasegawa's General Store, one of Hawaii's famous institutions, burned down in 1990 and already may be replaced by a new structure. I hope this delightful shopping landmark will be around when you get there.

Where to Stay

Stay for at least one night in Hana. Traveling within a tight budget? Try to reserve one of the fully furnished, not fancy but perfectly adequate housekeeping cabins (sleeps up to six, $15-$30 per night depending on the number of persons) next to **Waianapanapa State Park** (Department of Land and Natural Resources, State Division of Parks, 54 High St., Wailuku, HI 96793, 244-4354)—and stay several nights!

On the way into Hana, behind a Japanese gate on the left guarded by two stone lions, is the charming **Heavenly Hana Inn** (Box 146, Hana, Maui HI 96713, 248-8442, $85-$110). Around a common area designed in Japanese motif are four 2-bedroom garden suites, one in each corner of the building, with private bath and kitchenette, and screened-in lanai. Other comfortable alternatives managed by the inn include a beach cottage on Hana Bay and "the red barn," which is not a barn at all but a very roomy and homey cottage, next to Hasegawa's.

Hana Plantation Houses (P.O. Box 489, Hana, Maui, HI 96713, 800-657-7723 or 248-7248) has a wide variety of attractive units: the Lani Makaalae Studio ($80), very private with its own entrance to a tropical bath garden and jacuzzi tub/shower built into a deck under plumeria trees; Lani Too ($100), a two-bedroom cottage in Japanese-Balinese style; and three other units on a beautifully landscaped five-acre site. Situated on a secluded black sand beach, a mile from the center of Hana, are the **Waikoloa Beach Houses**: a two-bedroom cottage with the interior built of exotic woods ($195) and a separate, private sleeping room with outdoor private bath and no kitchen ($65).

The 19 private oceanview studios and one-bedroom apartments of the **Hana Kai-Maui Resort** condominiums (1533 Uakea Rd., P.O. Box 38, Hana, HI 96713, 248-8426 or toll-free 800-346-2772) only a few steps from a stony ocean beach. The lanais with lovely ocean views more than compensate for the plain rooms and lack of air-conditioning.

The **Hotel Hana-Maui**, an exclusive luxury retreat, costs over $450 per day for the least expensive room. The hotel was completely refurbished a few years ago to enhance its charm and elegance. In its garden setting, low-rise bungalows framed by orchids and plumeria reflect the Hawaii of a half century ago combined with plenty of contemporary pampering and activity choices. Three meals are included in the extravagant price. The hotel shuttles its guests over to lovely Hamoa Beach, west of Hana town, which anyone can use, except for the hotel's private facilities.

Above the Hana-Maui, Fusae Nakamura's **Aloha Cottages** (73 Keawa Place, P.O. Box 205, Hana, Maui, HI 96713, 248-8420, $60-$85), six simple, cozy two-bedroom units seem to have grown up together with surrounding papaya and banana trees. For your vacation pleasure, Stan and Suzanne Collins of **Hana Bay Vacation Rentals**, P.O. Box 318, Hana, Maui, HI 96713 (248-7727 or toll-free 800-657-7970) have gathered many home, cabin, and apartment choices in secluded shoreline or hillside locations.

Where to Eat
Besides the ultra-expensive **Hana Maui**, the only places to eat in Hana are **Tutu's**, for salads, sandwiches, and plate lunches, and the **Hana Ranch Restaurant**, on the hill across from the Post Office. From the take-out window, breakfast and lunch are inexpensive; inside, an all you can eat buffet lunch for $7.95 offers an excellent vari-

ety of meat, chicken, fish, vegetable, and salad servings
from 11:00 a.m. to 3:00 p.m or dinner (Friday and Saturday
only).

Itinerary Options

An alternative to driving to Hana is a 15-minute flight on
Aloha Island Air to Hana Airport (248-8208). Dollar Car
Rental (248-8237) will send a car to pick you up or Hana-
Maui Resort or Hana Kai-Maui Resort Condominiums will
be there with a minibus if you're a guest.

   Red Sand Beach is truly beautiful, tucked into the side
of Hana's Ka'uki Hill but dangerous to reach. From the
community center at the end of Hauoli Road, walk around
the hill on a clear, crumbly path down to the cove.
Horseback riding on the **Hana-Kaupo Coast** can be
arranged through Ohe'o Riding Stables, 248-7722; Hauoli
Lio Stables, 248-8435; Charley's Trail Rides and Pack Trips,
248-8209; the Hotel Hana Maui, 248-8211; and Adventures
on Horseback, 242-7445. Horseback riding will cost up to
$150 for a one-day trip including lunch.

   Kipahulu/Ohe'o Gulch: South of Hana, private lands
and roads conceal many heiau that Hawaiians must have
built in tropical terrain reminiscent of temples proliferating
in Guatemalan jungles. A terrible winding road through
gorgeous terrain brings too many tourists to large parking
lots near the Seven Sacred Pools that are neither "sacred"
nor "seven." Water cascades down Ohe'o Gulch through a
few dozen pools to the ocean along a path of rocky
ledges perfect for picnics and swimming. About a mile
beyond Ohe'o Gulch is Kipahulu, one of Hawaii's most
precious and beautiful valleys.

   The trip from Kipahulu to Kaupo or Ulupalakua Ranch
should only be attempted with four-wheel drive or on
foot. The pavement ends shortly beyond Kipahulu and
turns into a one-lane gravel road that skirts rocky cliffs and
dips steeply into gulches. (In winter, watch out for flash
floods.) The tin-roofed semi-ghost town of Kaupo is the
start of Kaupo Gap Trail. At the end of the road is lush
Ulupalakua Ranch, and a wine-tasting tour at Tedeschi
Winery awaits (if you didn't take one during Day 5).

MAUI'S SOUTHWEST COAST AND TRIP TO MOLOKAI

On the way back from Hana, pass marvelous views over the Keanae Peninsula and visit the Keanae Arboretum to see taro fields and rain forests up close. Have an early lunch in Paia or head directly to Kihei on Highway 350 and then Kihei Road for a swim and lunch on a sunny beach such as palm-fringed Kalama Park. Drive past the southwest coast's luxury Wailea Resort to beautiful Makena Beach for the remainder of the early afternoon. Return to Maui's airport with enough time to return your rental car and catch the last flight to Molokai at 4:40 p.m. Dry west Molokai, with its outstanding beaches, is slated for huge tourist developments. Southwest and northwest coasts hide picturesque beaches. East Molokai is still lush, rural, and mountainous.

Suggested Schedule

6:30 a.m.	Rise early for breakfast and check out. Head back to Paia. Stop at Uncle Harry's for some fresh banana bread.
8:30 a.m.	Visit Keanae Arboretum.
11:30 a.m.	Paia for lunch and shopping or head directly to Kihei for a snack at the beach.
1:00 p.m.	Drive past Kihei and Wailea beaches to Makena beaches. Option: If you have a four-wheel drive and snorkeling gear, head toward La Perouse Bay for snorkeling in the Ahini-Kinau Natural Reserve Area.
3:00 p.m.	Drive to the airport and return your rental car.
4:40 p.m.	Flight to Molokai.
7:00 p.m.	Check in at Molokai accommodations and dinner.
8:00 p.m.	Early to bed with an early morning ahead tomorrow.

Sightseeing Highlights

▲▲Uncle Harry's Roadside Stand—Operated by Harry Mitchell and his family, the stand (adjacent to the Wailua exit from the Hana Road) sells Hawaiian food, snacks, and souvenirs with a rare warmth and knowledge of old Hawaii.

▲▲Keanae Arboretum—This arboretum provides insight into the cultivation of taro, traditionally Hawaii's most important food crop. The arboretum also shows banana and sugarcane cultivation. An unmarked 1-mile trail, a little tough and often muddy, can be hiked from the end of the taro patches.

Follow the King's Trail of ancient Hawaiians who used to travel the southern shore to Hana down to Ahini-Kinau Nature Reserve and La Perouse Bay. See firsthand what the final phase of the struggle to preserve Hawaii's cultural and natural environment is all about. Catch glimpses of scarce wildlife: axis deer, wild turkeys, ring-necked pheasants, chukar, California valley quail, and Hawaii owl. In winter, pause on a grassy knoll and watch humpback whales perform in choppy channels between nearby islands. Walks or trail rides later in the day almost always will encounter a magical Maui sunset lighting up the ocean and the islands of Lanai, Kahoolawe, and Molokini.

▲▲▲Makena Beach—Down winding Wailea Alanui Road, the Makena Surf condos and the Maui Prince Resort emerged from a vast arid acreage of kiawe trees to follow the same patterns as the Wailea Resort next door. About 1.7 miles from Wailea Shopping Center on Makena Alanui Road, turn right to the white sands of Poolenalena Beach Park; another 2.3 miles beyond Wailea, Makena Alanui Road (an easy-to-drive dirt track) leads to a turnoff to the right past Red Hill to Makena Beach (the turnoff on the Wailea side of Red Hill is to Black Sands Beach). This road continues to Ahini-Kinau Nature Reserve, 2,000 acres of land and ocean with wonderful tidepools and coral reefs.

Getting to Molokai

Aloha Island Air and Panorama Air fly 9- to-18-seat Dash-7 turboprops to Molokai from Oahu and Maui with connections to all islands. Hawaiian Air runs 50-seat DH-7 aircraft. These flights land at Hoolehua Airport, near the center of the island, and shuttle vans will take you to your hotel or condo. From Hoolehua, Pacific Aviation International (800-245-9696 or 567-6128) offers an exciting 40-minute North Shore flight over Kalaupapa Peninsula (about $125), one of the best helicopter values in Hawaii. You could arrange to take this flightseeing excursion or a flight to Kalaupapa (see below) directly from the airport after landing.

The 118-foot *Maui Princess* (800-833-5800 or 533-6899 on Oahu, 661-8397 on Maui, and 553-5736 on Molokai) ferry from Lahaina takes about 75 minutes one way from Maui to Molokai and is excellent for a round-trip or one-way sightseeing, say, flying in from Honolulu or one of the neighbor islands and leaving Molokai by ferry to Maui. One-way fare is $25 for adults, $12.50 for children. Between December and May, when the trip gets a bit rough, you may spot some humpback whales. As you think about transportation alternatives, remember that just a day trip is barely enough time to see the best of Molokai, especially including a round-trip by ferry.

There is another small landing strip on Makanalua Peninsula that exclusively services Kalaupapa. You can fly directly from Honolulu or neighbor islands on Aloha Island Air, 25 miles across the Kaiwi Channel from Oahu and 9 miles across the Pacific to Kaanapali on Maui. Lanai is only 9 miles away across the Kalohi Channel.

Getting Around Molokai

There are no buses or public transportation on Molokai. Cab service (Teem Cab, 553-3433 or -3786 and Molokai Taxi 552-0041) will cost about $30 to east coast hotels and about the same price on a special bus to Kaluakoi Resort. Teem Cab also offers tours of several itineraries on the island.

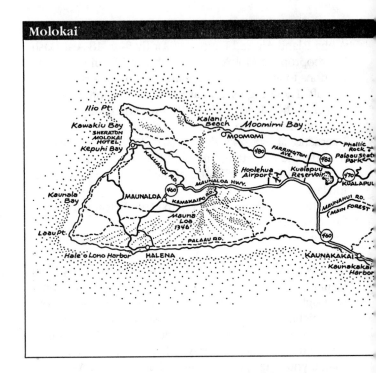

Half- and full-day tours can be arranged through Gray Line Molokai (567-6177), Roberts Hawaii (552-2751), and Molokai Off-Road Tours & Taxi (553-3369), for the lowest cost and best mountain and coastal tours. Most tours include the Kalaupapa Lookout, but be sure to take a tour that also includes the beautiful East Coast to Halawa Valley Overlook.

For off-the-beaten-track, four-wheel-drive sightseeing, such as the Waikoulu Lookout and Moomomi Beach, call Molokai Taxi (552-0041). In addition to Grayline and Roberts, Damien Molokai Tours (567-6171) will fly sightseers in and out of Kalaupapa Peninsula and arrange for a ground tour, all for $70.

For most people, the best plan is to rent a car at the airport so that you can drive yourself to sightseeing in all parts of the island. For some reason, Budget Rent-A-Car has had the lowest rates. Check rates at Dollar Car Rental (567-6118) and Tropical Rent-A-Car (567-6118), which

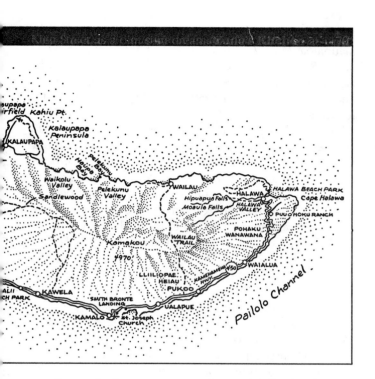

usually are the least expensive choices. Dollar has four-wheel-drive vehicles to rent at twice the cost of a compact rental. Per day rates vary seasonally from $28 for a standard shift subcompact to $32 for an automatic compact. Fill your tank on Saturday; gas stations are closed on Sundays.

If you bring your own bike, Molokai is ideal for two-wheeling on the east and west ends and a rough off-road ride with excellent scenery in the northwest and southeast. Bicyclers should take the morning boat (at 7:00 a.m.), the *Maui Princess*, and return the same day or preferably a few days later by boat, with bike transportation free and a low package rate for accommodations. Bring your own repair kit, too; there are no repair shops.

Where to Stay

Rooms, facilities, the beach and other beautiful nearby beaches, and the championship golf course at the

Kaluakoi Hotel and Golf Club (P.O. Box 1977, Maunaloa, Molokai 96770, 800-777-1700 or 552-2555) are an exceptional value at $100 to $125 per night. Ask about the golf package, which includes unlimited golf and a room for two for $250 per night. One of the better values, if it still exists, is the Colony Club plan, which includes all meals, bar drinks, one round of golf per person, two-night minimum for an oceanfront room at $470 in season. The new **Kaluakoi Villas** (P.O. Box 200, Maunaloa, Molokai, HI 96770, 800-525-1470) consist of 100 condominium units, studios, and one-bedroom suites, with oceanfront lanais, beautifully decorated with all amenities for $125 to $185. Next door, the **Ke Nani Kai** (P.O. Box 146, Maunaloa, Molokai, HI 96770, 800-888-2791 or 552-2761) condominium has 55 1- ($105 to $135) and 2-bedroom ($135 to $165) units with full kitchens and lanais looking across the seaside golf course and the beach. There's a very large pool, a jacuzzi, and two tennis courts. **Paniolo Hale** (P.O. Box 190, Maunaloa, Molokai, HI 96770, 800-367-2984 or 552-2731), also adjacent to the Kaluakoi, has 77 studio, 1- and 2-bedroom units with full kitchens, pool, paddle tennis court, and, of course, access to the golf course. Rates are about the same as the Ke Nani Kai. The minimum stay is three nights for all resort condominiums. **Hotel Molokai** (P.O. Box 546, Kaunakakai, Molokai HI 96748, 800-922-7866 or 553-5347) opened in 1966, has a tasteful Polynesian flavor, island-style 2-story wooden building, and rooms that run from $59 single or double rooms to upper floor oceanfront deluxe units for $125. The hotel has a lively open bar and restaurant (be sure to book a room away from the restaurant because of noise). The grounds are filled with flowers and coconut palms. A small pool facing the lagoon is a popular gathering place since there is no beach and no swimming (snorkeling is only decent).

Just past Kaunakakai on Highway 45, the **Pau Hana Inn** (P.O. Box 546, Kaunakakai, Molokai HI 96748, 800-922-7866 or 553-5342) is the oldest hotel on the island, very laid back, and mainly caters to *kamaainas*.

Its 39 cottage-type units recently were refurbished. Rates start at $45 single or double, and better units are $69 to $89 for two double or queen-size beds for up to four people. A 2-room oceanfront cottage rents for $85 to $125.

Aston Hotels and Resorts book and operate both the Hotel Molokai and the Pau Hana. Ask about a special package deal for two people that includes round-trip airfare on Panorama Air to Honolulu or Maui, two nights at the hotel, and two days of a Tropical rental car, at a cost of $125 per person.

Molokai Shores (Hawaiian Island Resorts, P.O. Box 212, Honolulu, HI 96810, 800-367-7042 or 553-5954), a condo located about 2 miles east of Kaunakakai, is a three-story 102-unit building with 1-bedroom units at $85 to $95 and 2-bedroom units at $125, all with full kitchens, pretty landscaping, a lagoon that is unswimmable (like everywhere else on the lagoon), the usual pool, a 9-hole putting green, and no bar or restaurant. Molokai Shores is an ideal place for a comfortable, pleasant, and restful vacation.

The 125-unit **Wavecrest Resort** (Star Rt. 155, Kaunakakai, HI 96748, 800-367-2980 or 558-8101), a condominium complex at mile marker 13 between Kamalo and Pukoo on the way to Halawa Bay, has 35 1- ($61-$76) and 2-bedroom ($86-$96) rentable suites, all with kitchens and ocean view. There's a pool, lighted tennis courts, and a general store on the premises. Ask about the package with a car for $107 to $117 per night per unit. In Pukoo, Diane and Larry **Swenson's Vacation Cottage** (P.O. Box 280, Kualapuu, Molokai, HI 96748, 567-9268), with living room, bedroom, kitchen, and bath, on a sandy swimming beach, is the best deal on the coast at $50 to $66. In a coconut grove with papayas, bananas, and mangos that you're welcome to pick, the cottage is within walking distance of lovely Pukoo Lagoon, a perfect swimming spot.

In Kamalo, **Herb and Marina Mueh's** (Star Rt., Box 128, Kaunakakai, HI 96748, 558-8236) cottage getaway on five acres has a minimum stay of two nights for a maximum of two adults at $50. Swimming beaches are about a 10-minute drive. The most outstanding rental unit on Molokai, near mile marker 20 en route to Halawa Valley, is **Hale Kawaikapu's cottage** at $85 a day double for a week (521-9202), on a beautiful private beach in a 250-acre tropical estate.

Papohaku State Park, fronting on one of Hawaii's most magnificent beaches, is the best place to camp on Molokai. **Palaau State Park** has become run-down but could be excellent if repaired. Other camping spots include **Kioea Park**, in the coconut grove, for $5 per day, with a permit from the Hawaiian Homelands Department in Hoolehua, 567-6104, and more crowded and noisy seaside camping four miles east of Kaunakakai at **O Ne Alii Park** and at **Beach Park and Wildlife Sanctuary**, both with county permits from County Parks and Recreation in Kaunakakai, 553-5141. To rent camping gear, contact Molokai Fish and Dive Corporation, 553-5926, in Kaunakakai.

Where to Eat

Depending on the weather and season, dine inside at the rustic **Banyan Terrace** around the enormous fireplace or outside under the huge banyan tree on the beach at the Pau Hana Inn (553-5342). Catch of the day and prime ribs are the two best choices, and dinner includes salad bar.

The food is simple and excellent at the Hotel Molokai's **Holo Holo Kai** (553-5347). Catch of the day tastes even better at sunset dining alfresco. Breakfasts at the hotel are legendary for their French toast (dipped in banana-egg batter) and pancakes with papaya. The hotel has its own garden where vegetables and fruit are grown for your dining enjoyment.

For inexpensive and very decent food, try funky **Jojo's Cafe** (552-2803, lunches and dinners) in Maunaloa. Fish is served every day (sometimes from frozen fish). For breakfast, **Kanemitsu Bakery** (553-5855) has some tables out back where you can order French toast made with delicious Molokai bread and then take out a loaf of Molokai cheese and onion bread for a picnic. A full breakfast here costs only $2.75. Buy your picnic plate lunch here with a side order of delicious Molokai French bread. From the outside, **Hop Inn** (553-5465) does not look very appetizing, but the lemon chicken, sizzling Mongolian beef, and other Chinese food is good.

One of the few recent additions to meal choices on Molokai, **Kualapuu Cookhouse** (567-6185, breakfasts, lunch, and dinner until 8:00 p.m.) in Kualapuu is located on Farrington Road. This is a perfect spot for breakfast or lunch en route to either Kalaupapa Lookout or the northwest coast beaches. All meals are priced under $8, and owner Nanette Yamashita bakes wonderful desserts.

Don't plan to eat after 9:00 p.m. at the **MidNite Inn** (553-3377) on Ala Malama in Kaunakakai, and don't dress up. You can expect very good catch of the day fish dinners for less than $8. This unpretentious restaurant gets rave reviews from many visitors to Molokai. Breakfasts are good and cheap. Bring your own bottle of wine for dinner. For a good sandwich for lunch or other health food items, **Outpost Natural Food** (553-3377) just off Ala Malama is open Sundays through Fridays from 9:00 a.m. to 6:00 p.m.

Farther east, 25 miles from Kaunakakai at mile marker 16, is the **Neighborhood Store 'n Counter** (558-8933) in Pukoo. If you haven't purchased food in Kaunakakai for a picnic lunch at Halawa Bay, the Neighborhood Store is the last store you'll see on the east end of the island. It has the largest plate lunch menu on the island including fresh fish, bento, sushi, and Hawaiian food.

Ohia Lodge (552-2555), the main dining room in Kaluakoi and the only elegant restaurant on the island, is one of the best. In addition to fresh fish, Oriental-style appetizers and entrées are a specialty. Vegetables, fruits, cheeses, and other selections in a salad buffet make a very healthful lunch choice. The restaurant's setting above the surf certainly is one of the most pleasant on the island. Every night there's music for dancing. The hotel's **Paniolo Broiler** is a good fish-to-steak restaurant.

Nightlife

Nightlife revolves around the **Pau Hana Bar** courtyard
with dancing under the sprawling banyan tree, a local
band, torchlights at the lagoon, and local people "talking
story." The bar gets a bit rowdy on the weekends. If you
prefer a quiet drink and island music, try the **Holoholo
Dining Room** of the **Hotel Molokai**, especially on
weekends. Check the bulletin board in the center of
town to see what's going on.

Itinerary Options

Whale-watching excursions run from January through
April on the Seabird Cruises, Inc.'s *Spirit of Windjammer*,
a 75-foot, 3-masted schooner out of Lahaina at 9:30 a.m.
(call 667-6834 or 800-843-8113). Or you can combine
your whale watching with snorkeling around Lanai on
Seabird Cruises' *Aikane III* (661-3643). Half-day trips
should cost no more than $75 and with increasing com-
petition may be as low as $45 off-season.

Also contact **Molokai Charters**, P.O. Box 1207,
Kaunakakai, Molokai, HI 96748, 443-5852.

MOLOKAI: KALAUPAPA

An all-day round-trip down from the 2,000-foot pali takes you to one of the most remote spots in Hawaii, the exile of lepers at Kalaupapa, where Father Damien devoted 16 years to helping about a thousand outcasts improve their tragic lives. After you return to the clifftop, take two short drives to the west and east ends for spectacular view points over the cliffs, visiting Palaau State Park and possibly Waikolu Overlook.

Suggested Schedule	
7:30 a.m.	Breakfast in Kaunakakai.
8:00 a.m	Drive past Kapuaiwa Royal Coconut Grove and Church Row on the road to Kualapuu and Kalaupapa Lookout.
8:30 a.m.	Head of mule trail for mule trip or walk down to Kalaupapa.
9:00 a.m	Start of mule ride from Kalae to Kalaupapa and tour of Makanalua Peninsula.
12:00 noon	Picnic lunch at Kalawao Park.
3:30 p.m.	From Kalaupapa, head for Palaau State Park.
4:30 p.m.	Option: Drive from Palaau Park to Waikolu Overlook.
6:00 p.m.	Return to Kaunakakai and freshen up for dinner.
8:30 p.m.	Enjoy a quiet evening at the Hotel Molakai's cocktail lounge.

Getting to Kalaupapa
Head west from Kaunakakai on Route 460, past cornfields and the startling contrast of dead trees. Continue up Route 470 through Kualapuu to the mule trail that switchbacks 1,600 feet down to Kalaupapa.

Just a few yards before the start of the mule trail, on the west side of the road, are the stables for the mule ride to Kalaupapa. The Rare Adventures/Molokai Mule Ride, P.O. Box 200, Kualapuu, HI 96757, 567-6088 or toll-free

800-843-5978 ($120), adds excitement to the trip down the 3-mile mountainside trail, 1,600 feet down through 26 switchbacks. Hiking down or up is not too difficult if you're in good physical condition. Otherwise it's tough coming back up. Riding or hiking down takes about 1½ hours. Hikers have to start ahead of the mules, by 8:30 a.m. at Kalae Stables. Mule riders leave at 9:00 a.m. and return to the stables by 4:00 p.m. A "hike-in" costs $30 including a pass to enter the peninsula, a picnic lunch, and a guided tour of the settlement.

The best tour deal in Hawaii is flying into Kalaupapa for $42 round-trip airfare with Richard Mark's Damien Molokai Tours, P.O. Box 1, Kalaupapa, Molokai, HI 96742, 567-6171. A 4-hour tour costs $22 per person (in addition to air-fare) and includes a visit to Kalawao, where you can see Father Damien's St. Philomena Church, the gravesites of Father Damien (his remains have been moved to Belgium) and Mother Marianne, and Siloama Church.

For all Kalaupapa tours, make reservations before arriv-ing on Molokai! One way or another, you have to pay to go down to Kalaupapa and make a specific booking for a tour and lunch. You can't simply hike down or enter Kalaupapa unescorted.

Sightseeing Highlights

▲▲**Kaunakakai**—This is the island's main town, which hasn't changed much since World War II. The island's pineapple plantations have closed down, jobs are scarce, and many Molokai workers commute to Maui every day on the *Maui Princess* to work at low-paying jobs. Ala Malama, the two-block main street running through Kaunakakai, is bordered by general stores, restaurants, a post office and court house, and the fabled Kanemitsu Bakery. At the end of the street, deep-sea fishing boats and the ferry leave from the concrete, one-half-mile-long Kaunakakai Wharf. The foundation of Kamehameha V's summer home is just to the west of the approach to the wharf, but there's not much to see. At the wharf, you can arrange for snorkeling or whale-watching excursions (Whistling Swan Charters, 553-5238) or other daylong sailing trips, for example, to

Lanai. Rent snorkeling gear from nearby Molokai Fish and Dive.

▲**Kapuaiwa Royal Coconut Grove**—The grove is only a few minutes drive to the west of Kaunakakai's center. It began with 1,000 trees planted in honor of High Chief Kapuaiwa, who became King Kamehameha V. The grove has thinned out considerably since then. Beware of walking under the royal coconut palms when the wind is blowing.

▲**Church Row**—Across Route 45 from the Coconut Grove, a half-dozen one-room churches and a mission school create a hive of interdenominational activity on Sunday morning, producing the island's only traffic jam.

▲▲▲**Kalaupapa Leper Colony**—Makanalua Peninsula, an isolated stretch of lava covering 12 square miles, surrounded by seas on three sides and sheer cliffs on the fourth side, became a prison for lepers starting in January 1866. Dumped off ships near the peninsula, lepers who survived the sea lived and died in unimaginable conditions in the most inaccessible place in the islands that the Hawaiian government could find—Kalaupapa. The settlement moved to Kalaupapa in 1888.

Father Damien de Veuster, a Catholic priest from Belgium, arrived to look after the victims of "Hansen's disease" in 1873. Sleeping under a tree until all residents of Kalaupapa had shelter, he converted St. Philomena chapel, built earlier by a visiting priest, into a hospital and also built another church. In April 1889, Father Damien died of Hansen's disease.

In the 1940s, the introduction of sulfone drugs arrested the spread of Hansen's disease. With the disease no longer contagious, the residents were free to leave Kalaupapa or voluntarily remain at the settlement, which had been declared a National Historic Park (remaining under state control). From a population of about 1,200 at the beginning of the century, the settlement today numbers about 60. Kalaupapa is a deeply moving experience that is definitely not for everyone. Minors under 16 are not allowed to enter the peninsula. Everyone else must have a permit, which is obtained by tour operators, all of whom are former patients. Advance reservations for any of the tours are essential. You can bring a camera (photos of residents are not allowed) and binoculars.

▲▲**Palaau State Park**—Off Route 470, high on a bluff overlooking Kalaupapa Peninsula and the ocean, a trail leads from the parking lot up a hill through beautiful ironwoods to Phallic Rock, where childless women came in hopes of receiving fertility. A second trail from the parking lot leads to an overlook behind a wall, with a perfect view of Kalaupapa and historical information to explain what you're seeing.

Itinerary Options

On Highway 460, a half mile south of its junction with Route 470, a dirt and gravel Forest Reserve four-wheel-drive road leads to the right (east). Drive nine miles to the **Sandalwood Measuring Pit**, a depression in the ground about the size of a sailing ship's hull used in the late nineteenth century by local Hawaiian chiefs to measure the amount of sandalwood stripped from local forests being shipped to haole traders. About two miles farther is **Waikolu Valley Lookout**, a spectacular view point over a 3,000-foot gorge. Just past the lookout is the gate to **Kamakou Preserve**, a 2,774-acre forest and bird conservation area established by the Nature Conservancy.

The Nature Conservancy owns a total of about 3,000 acres of mountain rain forest at the **Moomomi Dunes** near the west end of the island and in Pelekunu Valley/Kamakou Preserve along the north coast. In Hoolehua, take a right on Route 481 (Puupeelua Avenue) and then left on Farrington Avenue (Route 480). At the end of paved Route 480, a dirt road continues for 2.2 miles to a fork. Take the right fork and follow it a half mile to **Moomomi Beach** where swimming, snorkeling, and unofficial camping are good. You can hike in the preserve or drive in with a four-wheel-drive vehicle. Be sure to get maps and information first. Tours can be arranged by contacting the **Nature Conservancy** (P.O. Box 40, Kaunakakai, HI 96757, 567-6680). For guided hiking in the preserve and all of the other beautiful parts of Molokai, contact Ken Gibson, **Discover Molokai**, P.O. Box 123, Moanaloa, Molokai, HI 96770, 552-2975.

MOLOKAI: HALAWA VALLEY TO WEST MOLOKAI

Drive along the south shore past mile after mile of historic sites and occasional good beaches to spectacular views of the Halawa Valley. Walk in the valley to Moaula Falls and picnic at the pool below the falls. Then, for a complete contrast, drive to the west end of Molokai to end the day watching the sunset over the island's second-best beach at the Kaluakoi Resort or from beautiful Papohaku Beach, stretching wide for about a mile along the lush coast (one day to be part of a huge resort but still open to the public).

Suggested Schedule

7:00 a.m.	Breakfast and shop for a picnic lunch in Kaunakakai.
8:00 a.m.	Start the south shore drive to Halawa Valley.
8:15 a.m.	Kalokoeli Fish Pond.
8:45 a.m.	Iliiliopae Heiau.
10:00 a.m.	Arrive at Halawa Valley Lookout.
10:15 a.m.	Drive down the valley, park, and walk to the pool at the base of Moaula Falls.
11:30 a.m.	Swim in the pool and sun on the rocks.
12:00 noon	Picnic lunch.
1:30 p.m.	Return to your car and drive to Kaluakoi Resort. (Option: from the resort, take a tour of Molokai Wildlife Park; a 3:30 p.m. tour leaves from the Kaluakoi Resort.)
5:30 p.m.	Sunset from Papohaku Beach.
6:30 p.m.	Dinner at the oceanside Paniolo Broiler.
8:00 p.m.	Return to Kaunakakai or linger for the evening at the Kaluakoi Resort.

Travel Route
Highway 45 runs from Kaunakakai along the south and east shore for 30 miles to the Halawa Valley. Virtually each mile has a historic site of greater or lesser importance, from major ancient Polynesian sites like Iliiliopae Heiau and the 58 fish

ponds to the marker where aviators Smith and Bronte landed awkwardly but unharmed in a clump of trees. Plan on a
1- to 2-hour drive, depending on your pace, on a road that
defies haste. The paved two-lane road twists and turns for
nine miles as you ascend the green slopes to Puu O Hoku
(Hill of Stars) Ranch and Lodge, dotted with French
Charolais cattle. There are great views across Pailolo Channel
to Maui and Mount Haleakala as you round the hairpin turn
to the overlook into the four-mile-long Halawa Valley with
its two magnificent waterfalls plummeting to the stream
below. The road zigzags down the ridge in the broad, deep
green valley, backed by cliffs.

Sightseeing Highlights

▲▲**Kalokoeli Fish Pond**—Molokai is renowned in Hawaii
for its remarkably advanced fish ponds, which may have
existed as early as the thirteenth century. Built on the shallow southeastern shores, the ponds were formed of stone or
coral in just the right spots for tides to keep the waters in the
ponds circulating but not too strong to wreck the fish ponds'
walls. Small openings in the walls let small fish in with the
water but did not allow fattened fish to escape.

▲▲**Iliiliopae Heiau**—Just east of Kamalo, on the *mauka*
side of the road, is one of Hawaii's largest and most sacred
temples. This heiau once covered more than five acres, con-
sisting of four terraces, 150 feet wide and 50 feet tall. Legend
says that the stones used to build this heiau were carried
from Wailau Valley and fitted together in one night. Human
sacrifices were performed here. It is said that this heiau was
a school of sorcery for *kahuna* from other islands. Since this
is a sacred site, see it either with the wagon tour or with per-
mission from Pearl Petro (P.O. Box 125, Kaunakakai,
Molokai, HI 96748, 558-8113; also see Itinerary Options:
Molokai Wagon Ride). Or check at your hotel desk for clear-
ance.

▲▲▲**Halawa Valley**—This valley is believed to be the first
settlement on Molokai, dating back to the seventh century.
There are two waterfalls at the end of the valley: Moaula
Falls, an upper and lower falls with a pool at the base of the
lower falls for swimming; and Hipuapua, a single waterfall

with a pool at the base. When you reach the valley floor, a narrow dirt side road turns sharply to the left in front of the small green church to the trailhead up to Moaula Falls, while the main road runs a few hundred yards to the county park and beach. Leave your car across from the church. Take the road for half a mile to its end, passing several houses on your left along the way. There a foot trail begins. Walk about 100 yards to a row of rocks across the trail and a stone wall and turn right down to the stream. Cross both forks of the stream at the *easiest and safest place* (you probably will have to wade across the stream). The trail goes uphill perpendicular to the stream. Look for an orange mark on a tree where the trail continues through heavy grass and mango groves (deliciously ripe from March to October) to a fork: right to the beach, or left to the lower falls following a white plastic pipe and white arrows. (You probably will have to wade across the stream.) If the stream is too broad and deep to cross, take the trail to the left near the green church, head upstream following old stone walls and a white water pipe to a fork a short distance past the Hipuapua Stream branching off Halawa Stream. The left-hand trail goes to the lower pool, the steep right-hand fork to the upper pool.

▲▲**The Kaluakoi Resort**—The biggest and best hotel and only resort on the island, the 117-room Kaluakoi Hotel and Golf Club on 29 acres started out in 1977 as the Sheraton Molokai. Situated 15 miles from the airport, the hotel is part of the 6,700-acre Kaluakoi Resort. Your own car is essential for sightseeing. The hotel's very nicely decorated rooms are in 32 1- and 2-story villas around the grounds. The hotel has a small swimming pool, four lighted tennis courts, two restaurants and a lounge, and an 18-hole championship golf course (552-2739 or 552-2555). A breeze constantly blows at Kepuhi Beach in front of Kaluakoi Resort. Swim with caution, especially in winter when waves get rough. Plan for dinner by the open glass doors at the Ohia Lodge in Kaluakoi Hotel. Live bands play top 40 music for dancing in the Ohia Lodge every evening.

Molokai Ranch Wildlife Park—You can take a "safari" in an air-conditioned van to see more than a dozen African animals roaming the Molokai Ranch. This 90-minute tour costs

$30 for adults, $20 for children, and can be booked at the Kaluakai Hotel, 552-2555. This ranch along Highway 460 was originally the royal ranch of the Kamehamehas.

Itinerary Options

Most of the west side of Molokai is owned or leased by the company that purchased Molokai Ranch Ltd. This arid, high tableland, largely used for grazing and growing cattle feed and on hold for inevitable future development, contains the Kalaukoi Resort; the former Dole company town of Maunaloa and its few interesting shops; and a fringe of "hidden" beaches, some very scenic, that are mostly difficult to reach, which makes them all the more appealing to adventuresome travelers.

Beaches: The island's best beaches are scattered around the west side. The white sands of **Poolau Beach**, about a half mile northwest of Kaluakoi Hotel, are an excellent place for camping and surfing. Obtain a county camping permit (553-5141) at the County Parks Division in Kaunakakai. The loveliest beach on the west coast is **Kawakui**, about 20 miles from Kaunakakai, down a dirt road off Route 46 to the end of a point north of the Kaluakoi Hotel. Swimming and snorkeling in the cove are good, and camping is wonderful. A permit is required only on weekends from Molokai Ranch (552-2767).

Papohaku Beach, two miles south of the Kaluakoi Hotel, is a marvelous, scenic beach extending for three miles, with rest rooms and showers, camping by county permit, and good swimming with caution! About 1½ miles past Papohaku is **Pohakuloa Beach** in a cove with excellent swimming and an outdoor shower.

Molokai Wagon Ride: One of the newest tours on Molokai is a horse-drawn wagon ride to the Iliiliopae Heiau, where a guide explains the historical background. Then the wagon continues to the Mapulehu Mango Grove, the largest in Hawaii and perhaps even the world, in Mapulehu, at the 15½ mile marker on the *makai* side. Afterward, the wagon heads to the beach for a Molokai-style barbecue, which means a wonderful party. Cost is $35 for adults, $17.50 for children. Contact Larry Helm, 567-6773 or 558-8380.

LANAI

The silhouette of a razor-backed ridge covered with
Norfolk pines stands out as your plane approaches Lanai.
A profusion of great red gulches descends from the
Munro Trail, which is your first destination as quickly as
you can get into a four-wheel drive in Lanai City. To the
southwest is a broad crescent of white sand, Hulopoe
Beach on Manele Bay, your second spectacular destination. Farther to the west, where enormously high seacliffs
frame the coastline, is Kaunolu Village, where some of
the archipelago's most sacred ancient sites are scattered
across a rocky point above the sea. The area was one of
Kamehameha the Great's favorite recreation spots.

Suggested Schedule

5:30 a.m.	Early breakfast at the Midnite Inn.
6:00 a.m.	Drive to the airport.
6:45 a.m.	Flight to Lanai.
7:40 a.m.	Oshiro's Service Station picks you up at the Lanai Airport.
8:00 a.m.	Rent a four-wheel drive and buy picnic supplies in Lanai City.
8:30 a.m.	Head for Munro Trail.
11:00 a.m.	Arrive at the Hale Lookout.
12:00 noon	Drive to Manele and Hulopoe bays.
1:00 p.m.	Swim and picnic lunch at Hulopoe Bay.
2:30 p.m.	Head west to explore Kaunolu.
5:15 p.m.	Drive to the airport.
5:40 p.m.	Return to Molokai.
6:30 p.m.	Clean up at your hotel for dinner.
7:30 p.m.	A relaxing dinner and a last evening on Molokai.

Orientation

After his bloody invasion of Lanai, Kamehameha returned
years later for summer vacations and fishing at Kaunolu.
Following the path of missionaries in the early 1800s, in

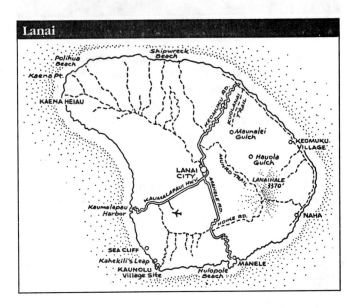

Lanai

the 1850s Mormons arrived to establish a "City of Joseph." Their leader, Walter Gibson, bought up prime Lanai land, was excommunicated in a period of turmoil, and the Mormons left for Laie to establish their church on Oahu's north shore. Landholdings of Gibson's heir were expanded and converted to ranching and then sold to the Baldwin family of Maui. In 1921, the Baldwins sold most of the island to Jim Dole, who spent millions to develop Lanai as a pineapple plantation. The island only has 30 miles of paved roads and a few thousand residents—a mixture of Hawaiians, Filipinos, Japanese, Koreans, Chinese, and Caucasians, almost all of whom live in Lanai City.

In 1990, Lanai turned a historic corner and began to shut down its pineapple plantation and become an exclusive resort island. Hawaii's sixth-largest island now offers two world-class resorts. Lanai today is the biggest "undiscovered" secret in Hawaii, a getaway offering a wealth of vacation possibilities for outdoor activities, touring, and dining. Lanai is a golfers' paradise, with two superb championship courses. Besides exotic flora and spectacular vistas, there is abundant wildlife in the mountains.

Getting to and around Lanai

The island is serviced by Hawaiian Airlines and Aloha Island Air. Aloha Island Air has a flight at 6:45 a.m. from Molokai to Lanai. The return flight leaves Lanai at 5:40 p.m. for Molokai. The fare is reasonable. Lanai Airport is out in the pineapple fields, about four miles southwest of Lanai City. There's nothing out there. Unless you have reservations at one of the two resorts on Lanai, make prior arrangements for Oshiro's Service Station (565-6952) to pick you up. With only 30 miles of paved roads, you need a four-wheel drive to tour the island. Oshiro's Service Station, 565-6952, and Lanai City Service, Inc., 565-7277, rent them for $75 to $85 a day. Oshiro's also will provide a guided tour of 2 to 4 hours to the island's many off-the-beaten-track coastal and mountain areas.

The other way to get to Lanai is an all-day excursion with Trilogy Excursions (661-4743 or toll-free 800-874-2666) from Lahaina, Maui to Hulupo'e Bay, Lanai. The trip includes superb snorkeling, a wonderful barbecued lunch, and a tour around the island in an air-conditioned van. You can arrange for a stopover on Lanai, to return the next day or later on. Cost is $139 for adults, $70 for children.

Sightseeing Highlights

▲▲**Lanai City**—A plantation town below the mountains, Lanai City has a delightful climate because of its 1,600-foot altitude. The island's population of about 2,500, the majority Filipinos, lives in homes painted all colors of the rainbow, surrounded by colorful gardens of fruits, vegetables, and flowering shrubs and plants. The Pine Isle Market and Richards Shopping Center, next to each other on Eighth Street, can take care of your picnic needs.

At the center of the town is a village green with its towering Norfolk pine trees surrounded by a cluster of country stores, churches, a bakery, and an old-fashioned soda fountain. Dahang's Bakery serves fresh bread and pastry in the morning and otherwise is a budget luncheonette of the burgers-and-french-fries variety. S & T Property Inc., next door to Dahang's Bakery on 7th Avenue in Lanai City, is a '50s-style soda fountain complete with swivel chairs and burgers (good ones, too). If you don't mind video machines flashing on and off, this is the place for a budget breakfast or lunch.

Built in the 1920s for guests of the Dole Company, the white wood frame Hotel Lanai (828 Lanai Avenue, Lanai, HI 96763, 565-7211) sits atop a grassy knoll surrounded by Norfolk pines. The knotty pine dining rooms with fireplaces fit the temperate climate. The big veranda and its bar are the town's meeting place. Ten small rooms in two wings of the building, all with bathroom and shower, feel quite homey and comfortable. They rent for $75 for two persons.

▲▲▲**The Munro Trail**—This trail leads to Lanaihale (The Hale), the highest point (3,370 feet). The trail to The Hale cuts through tall eucalyptus stands, shaggy ironwoods, and Cook Island and Norfolk pines, perfect green cone shapes as far as the eye can see. Before leaving town, ASK ABOUT ROAD CONDITIONS! A recent heavy downpour can turn jeep trails into impassable quagmires. Before leaving, rent snorkeling gear at Lanai City Service for the trip to Manele Bay and Hulupoa, and pick up your picnic lunch in Lanai City. Head north 1½ miles out of Lanai City on Route 44 (Keomoku Road) toward Shipwreck Beach, turn right on the first major gravel road (marked by a sign), then turn left at the first fork and again at the next fork. The trail is 8.8 miles one way, easy for a four-wheel drive, except when it's very wet and rutted. When you arrive at the crest of The Hale, ahead of the afternoon clouds, you can see all of the Hawaiian Islands except Kauai. From the trail, head straight to Hoike Road, which connects with Manele Road and turn left for Manele Bay and Hulopoe.

▲▲**Manele Bay/Hulopoe Bay and Beach**—Manele Bay is a splendid small boat anchorage with local and tour boats, mainly from Maui. Manele and crystal-clear Hulopoe Bay are a Marine Life Conservation District with some of the best snorkeling in the state. The palm-fringed white sands of Hulopoe Beach are picture-perfect. Six of the best camping sites in the state, with shower facilities, charge a $5 registration fee and a $5 per person fee, payable to the Koele Company, P.O. Box L, Lanai City, 565-6661.

▲▲▲**Kaunolu**—At the end of a long dry gulch on the southwestern tip of Lanai is a fishing village surrounded by Halulu Heiau, a sacred refuge where kapu breakers sought the protection of temple priests and their gods. The village contains the remains of Kamehameha's house. Across the rocky beach, past the remains of a canoe shed, climb to the heiau site, with mortarless walls up to 30 feet high, commanding a view of the surrounding cliffs and the village. This national landmark contains the ruins of over eighty houses, stone shelters, and graves. Across Kaunolu Bay is Halulu Heiau, with a commanding view of the area. Nearby, from Kahekili's Leap, as a test of their courage, warriors would plunge over the 60-foot cliff and a 15-foot outcropping below into 12 feet of water. On the right is a less famous but even higher leap, above Kolokolo Cava.

Itinerary Options

From Maui, the best way to visit Hulopoe Beach is aboard the 50-foot *Trilogy* trimaran, which costs $125 for a full day of snorkeling, picnicking, and local sightseeing. Call 661-4743 or 800-874-2666 to book a departure from Lahaina Harbor.

Koele Lodge and Manele Bay Hotel: Their restaurants, landscaping, and sports attractions add a whole new dimension to vacationing on Lanai. The Lodge at Koele, one mile from Lanai City, is designed like an elegant country inn. The kitchens of both the Lodge and Manele Bay draw on ten acres of organic gardens.

The Lodge is only 20 minutes from its sister resort at Manele Bay. The 250-room Manele Bay's contemporary architecture and decor offers a complete resort experience on Lanai. Gentle waves provide excellent snorkeling. All of the 250 villas and suites of the Manele Bay Hotel face the ocean. Scuba diving, snorkeling, kayaking, and sailing are available to guests in this water sports paradise. Jack Nicklaus designed the challenging 18-hole oceanfront golf course, the island's third, newly opened.

Rates at the Lodge and the Manele Bay Hotel are appropriately high: single or double occupancy ranges from $275 to $425 and up. For reservations, call 800-223-7637 or 800-321-4666.

South of Lanai City: The most likely direction for leaving Lanai City is south on Route 441 to Manele Bay and Hulopoe Bay. Start with the fascinating **Luahiwa Petroglyphs**, about a mile off Manele Road (Route 441) accessed on dirt pineapple field roads, near a high voltage shack below a water tower. These petroglyphs are some of the best in the islands, comparable to Puako on the Big Island. (Get clear, specific directions in Lanai City before setting out.) **Kaumalapau Harbor**, six miles to the southwest at the end of Route 44, a good two-lane highway, is worth visiting mainly to see the 1,000-foot pali on either side and for the detour to **Kaunolu Village**. The turnoff to Kaunolu is a paved road to the left just past the airport road which soon becomes a very rough road through pineapple fields.

Northeast of Lanai City: Gorgeous **Polihua** may be too windswept for some tastes, but it is well worth the buffeting. **Shipwreck Beach** is a beachcomber's delight, with some petroglyph carvings as a bonus. Leave Lanai City on Route 44 to the northeast for an adventuresome drive on a paved road through arid countryside to the beach. When the pavement ends and divides into two, take the road to the left through kiawe trees. A dirt track parallels the coast for plenty of coastal hiking or four-wheel driving. Protected by coral reefs but swept by strong currents, hulks of ships driven into the reefs are still visible. Stay out of the water in this area—it's dangerous!

To the north of the point where the dirt road ends is a group of **petroglyphs** carved on a pile of brown boulders near the beach. To the south is the ghost town of **Keomuku**, a sugar town abandoned in 1903 and mostly covered with vegetation.

Heading northwest, the **Garden of the Gods**, an unusual conglomeration of lava and multicolored boulders near Kanepuu, with a strange sculptural beauty, is reached by a graded and then ungraded pineapple road. (The boulders may be hard to find if overgrown with vegetation.) Continue on this rugged jeep trail to **Polihua Beach**, a wide, white sand strand with good swimming and outstanding fishing.

THE BIG ISLAND: HILO

Take an early morning flight from Molokai to Hilo via
Honolulu, arriving early enough to have practically a full
day in Hilo. Rain or shine, the Bay City is an interesting,
small tropical city that is slowly changing from a sugar
port to a service economy. The capital of the world's
tropical flower industry is a much better gateway to the
Big Island than Kailua-Kona if you wish to first experience the island's history and tropical character.

Suggested Schedule	
7:00 a.m.	Early breakfast and check out of Molokai hotel.
7:55 a.m.	Flight to Hilo.
9:30 a.m.	Arrive at General Lyman airport and rent a car.
10:30 a.m.	Check into Hilo accommodations.
11:00 a.m.	Stop at the Hawaii Visitor's Bureau before exploring the town.
1:00 p.m.	Lunch.
2:00 p.m.	Visit the Lyman Mission House and Museum.
3:00 p.m.	Visit Nani Mau Gardens.
7:00 p.m.	Dinner and Hilo nightlife.

Getting to the Big Island
Interisland airlines take you in about 30 minutes to Hilo
on the east or to Kailua-Kona on the west. Fly from
Molokai on the Hawaiian Airlines flight leaving Molokai
at 7:55 a.m., with a change of planes in Honolulu,
departing Honolulu at 8:55 a.m. and arriving in Hilo at
9:30 a.m. General Lyman Field in Hilo also has interisland jet service. Once the island's main airport, Lyman
has yielded to Kailua-Kona's Keahole Airport, which is
the main landing facility on the Big Island.

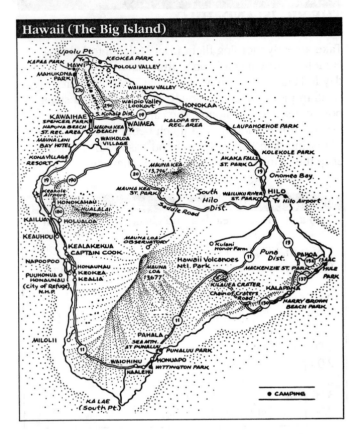

Hawaii (The Big Island)

Getting Around

It's a $12 cab fare for the 9-mile ride into town, and there's no bus service. To explore Hilo's historic sites, take a self-guided walking tour in the area between Kinoole Street, Furneaux Lane, Kamehameha Avenue, and Waianuenue Avenue. To explore outside of Hilo, Kailua-Kona, and Hawaii Volcanoes National Park, it's best to rent a car. You can use the Hele-On bus system to get anywhere you want to in the Hilo Bay area or north-south to various botanical gardens for only 75 cents, but it's time-consuming. The intraisland buses, Mass Transportation Agency/MTA, 935-8241, are among the best transportation values in the United States and a great way to meet interesting people. It's only 4 hours by

bus from Hilo to Kailua-Kona, but traveling by bus eliminates seeing the island's byways. The Hele-On Bus provides cross-island service Monday through Friday from
Hilo to Kailua-Kona via Hawaii Volcanoes National Park,
$6 for the cross-island run. The twice-daily round-the-
island trip costs $7. You can hail the bus from anywhere
along the roadside. There are daily buses from Hilo north
to Honokaa and Waimea. In Hilo, the Banyan Shuttle Bus
makes two round-trips (one in the morning and one in
the midafternoon) stopping at most of the visitor's attractions.

When renting a car, aim for a flat weekly rental rate
with unlimited mileage. The daily rate should be around
$17.95 (winter) and $14.95 (summer), returning the car
back in Hilo seven days later. Pick your car up at or near
the airport when you arrive. If you want a car in Hilo,
package it with a night at the Hilo Hotel for maximum
economy. Otherwise, your best choices are: Phillips's U-
Drive, Hilo—935-1936, Kona—329-1730; Robert's Hawaii
Rent-A-Car, Hilo—935-2858; United Car Services, Hilo—
935-2115, Kona—329-3411; Tropical Rent-A-Car, Hilo—
935-3385, Kona—329-2437; Ugly Duckling, Kona—329-
2113; Rent and Drive, Inc., Kona—329-3033; American
International Rent-A-Car, Hilo—935-1108, Kona—329-
2926; National Rent-A-Car, Hilo—935-0891, Kona—329-
1674; Dollar Rent-A-Car, Hilo—961-6059, Kona—329-
2744 (jeeps, too); Avis, Hilo—935-1290, Kona—329-1745;
Hertz, Hilo—935-2896, Kona—329-3566; and Budget
Rent-A-Car, Hilo—935-6878, Kona—329-8511 (jeeps, too).

Tour bus companies offer standardized rates. Jack's
Tours, Inc. (Kona, 329-2555; Hilo, 961-6666) offers a circle island tour for $40; likewise, Akamai Tours (329-
7324). Gray Line Hawaii (Kona, 329-9337; Hilo, 935-2835),
Hawaii Resorts Transportation (885-7484), and other
companies provide round-the-island, half-day and full-
day tours. Ask about van tours of Waipio ($30) and Kona
($30) and Mauna Kea ($50). Hawaiiana Resorts
Transportation will even put you on a horseback tour of
Waipio for $65. Tours are available to each major sight-
seeing attraction on the island: Hawaii Volcanoes

National Park, Waipio Valley, Parker Ranch, Kailua-Kona, the Hawaii Tropical Botanical Garden, and Nani Maui Gardens.

Consider flightseeing—a thrilling helicopter tour, second to none in Hawaii. Take off from Hilo's General Lyman Field (which is cheaper for volcano flights) or a helicopter pad near the Waikaloa Resort along Highway 19 and fly over Mauna Loa, volcano scenery, Puna and Kau, Kealakekua Bay and the City of Refuge, Kailua-Kona and the Keauhou-Kona Coast, Waimea and North Kohala, Waipio and the Hamakua Coast. A two-hour round-the-island tour of a Kilauea Tour costs about $300 per person. Contact: Kenai Air Hawaii (800-622-3144 or 329-7424) or Papillion Helicopters (800-562-5641 or 885-5995).

Most coast roads are ideal for cycling. The Saddle Road, roads to Waimea, and Hilo to Hawaii Volcanoes National Park are hard pedaling. Bicycles rent for $3 per hour or $10 per day. Rent bicycles at Ciao Activities in Hilo (969-1717) or Kona (326-4177) or at Dave's Triathlon Shop in Kona (329-4522). An easier and fun way to see the Kona or Hamakua coast (in the dry season) is by moped from Kona Fun 'n Sun, 329-6068; Freedom Scoots, 329-2832; or Rent Scootah, 329-3250. Mopeds rent for $5 per hour, $25 per day, or $125 per week.

Sightseeing Highlights
▲▲▲**Hilo**—Savor the 1940s feel of a few square blocks of frontier-style old wooden buildings whose elegantly trimmed facades and metal roofs stream rain daily. Seeing nurseries with commercially grown orchids and anthuriums, the city's chief crop (although the anthurium capital actually is nearby Pahoa in the Puna District), is a must for visitors.

A downtown revival is under way (retarded by a stalled national economy in 1991-92). The few sightseeing attractions in Hilo appeal to very particular tastes.
▲▲**Rainbow Falls**—Rainbow Drive, off Waianuenue Avenue, at Wailoa River State Park, offers memorable

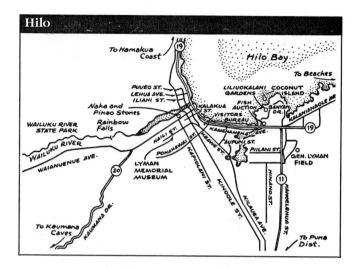

Hilo

views around 9:00 to 10:00 a.m. when rainbows rise in the morning mist. Up the road are the Boiling Pots, water bubbling up from lava beds. Watch for the signs.

▲▲**Banyan Drive**—A drive along the waterfront is hard to miss, since the banyan-shaded thoroughfare passes Hilo's prime hotels. Each tree has been named for a celebrated American, like Babe Ruth, Amelia Earhart, or Cecil B. DeMille, as shown on plaques in front of the trees.

▲**Liliuokalani Gardens**—Located on Waiakea Peninsula at the north end of Banyan Drive, this garden has 30 acres of colorful flowers and greenery including a Japanese garden with pagodas, lanterns, ponds, bridge, and ceremonial teahouse. This is one of the largest such gardens outside of Japan. The Nihon Japanese Cultural Center, 123 Lihiwai Street, 989-1133, overlooks Liliuokalani Gardens and contains many authentic Japanese treasures, an art gallery, tearoom, and restaurant. Check on special events. The gardens are always open, and admission is free.

▲**Richardson's Beach**—On Hilo Bay's south shore is Hilo's best beach for views of the bay and the best beach in the area for swimming, snorkeling, surfing, and fishing. Richardson Ocean Center, 935-3830, an oceanographic museum, is located next to the beach a quarter

mile beyond the end of Kalanianaole Avenue. Admission
is free. The center is open from 9:00 a.m. to 5:00 p.m.

▲▲**The Lyman Mission House and Museum**—In a
restored Mission House that was built in 1839, you'll see
handsome handmade koa mantels and doors, ohia wood
furniture from the 1850s, portraits, and family china. The
museum was established by members of the Lyman family
in 1932, 100 years after their arrival as missionaries in Hilo.
The Mission House, listed in the State and National
Registers of Historic Places, was built in 1839 and later
restored to its original appearance and furnishings. Watch
for special events at the museum on local history and culture, folklore, and the arts. The museum's Hawaiian and
ethnic exhibits, volcanic and mineral exhibit, large Pacific
shell collection, and Oriental exhibits are well worth the
visit. They are open daily except Sunday, from 10:00 a.m.
to 4:00 p.m. Admission fee is $3.50 for adults, $2.50 for
children 12 to 18, $1.50 for children 6 to 11. Located at 276
Haili Street, 935-5021.

▲**Naha Stone**—Standing in front of the County Library on
Waianuenue Avenue, this is the bigger of two stones (the
other is the Pinao Stone) that in ancient days stood before
the temple of Pinao near the library site. The Naha Stone
was used by Hawaiians to prove the legitimacy of heirs to
the Naha lineage. He who could move the stone would
become king. The one who overturned it would conquer
all the islands. According to legend, Kamehameha the
Great overturned the stone while still a young boy. (Yes, it
weighs about a ton!)

▲▲**Nani Mau Gardens**—Three miles south of Hilo, 1½
miles off Route 11 at 421 Makalika Street, 959-3541, these
20 acres grow all the varieties of trees (coffee, macadamia,
and fruit), plants (orchids, ginger, and hibiscus), and
unusual Hawaiian herbs and flowers that make the island
famous. Also visit the Japanese garden, miniature lake, and
herb garden. Open daily from 8:00 a.m. to 5:00 p.m. (with
a change of ownership, the admission charge has jumped
to $6 but is still worth it). An alternative is to wait until
tomorrow and see the Hawaii Tropical Botanical Garden
on the way north to the Hamakua Coast.

Where to Stay

A lush garden setting full of fruit trees in a quiet neighborhood makes the 18-unit **Dolphin Bay Hotel** (333 Ilahi Street, Hilo 96720, 935-1466) everyone's favorite little hotel on the Big Island. The hotel has large, nicely furnished studios, 1- and 2-bedroom apartments, full kitchens and tub-shower combinations. Singles range from $39 to $63 and doubles $49 to $79.

Robert and Sandra Woodward took over the Old Lanikai Hotel across from the Dolphin Bay and transformed it into **Wild Ginger Inn** (100 Puveo St., Hilo, HI 96720, 935-5566 or 800-822-1887), a serene alternative to more expensive hotels in Hilo. The $45 single and double (nonsmoking) rooms include continental breakfast. A resurrected Sheraton with 14 acres of very pleasant grounds, bayside **Waiakea Villas** (400 Hualani Street, Hilo, HI 96720, 800-367-6062 or 961-2841), a condominium hotel complex with 147 rooms in low-rise buildings has large studio units with kitchenettes for $75 to $85. The hotel has a swimming pool, a restaurant, and a great bakery (Kay's).

Hilo's bed-and-breakfast accommodations compare favorably with any place on the island. Patty Oliver's **Seaside Studio** (961-6178) is especially attractive for families and large groups. Patty's three-bedroom oceanfront house with a private beach, tidepools, private lanai, rents for $55 for 1 or 2 people. Surfers should contact Evonne Bjornen to stay at **Hale Kai** (111 Honalii Pali, Hilo, HI 96720, 935-6330), overlooking one of the best surfing spots on the island, Honalii Surfing Beach. Rates are about $70, including a delicious, hearty breakfast. The **Hilo Hukilau Hotel**, 126 Banyan Way, 96720, 935-0821 or 800-367-7000, has single or double rooms, standard to deluxe, for $55 to $70. Located bayfront at the far end of Banyan Drive, they're on a side street fronting on Reed's Bay. The 139 rooms are small and plain, but lanais overlook lush gardens. The **Hilo Hotel**, 142 Kinoole Street, 96720, 961-3733, across from Kalakaua Park is as basic (and clean), with or without kitchens, as you'll find in Hawaii. Rooms have telephones. Ask for the standard ($49 per day) or deluxe ($62-$68) room with car. Otherwise, single or double standard and deluxe rooms cost $38 and $49 for one or two persons. **Hawaii Naniloa Hotel**, 93 Banyan Drive, 969-3333 or 800-367-5360, $80 to $90, referred to locally as the "Queen of Banyan Drive," is a high-rise right on the water, with beautiful grounds and a very attractive swimming pool area, spacious lobby, large comfortably furnished rooms, all recently refurbished. For those who prefer to stay overnight north of Hilo, try **Ishigo's Inn B&B** (963-6128) in Honomu Village on the road to Akaka Falls State Park. Wake up to fresh pastries from Ishigo's bakery downstairs and then head up the hill to the park.

Where to Eat

A restaurant acquiring a reputation for Pacific Rim cuisine, **Lehua's Bay City Bar & Grill** (11 Waianuenue Avenue, one block from Keawe, 935-8055) serves imaginative sauces and seasonings combined with fresh local ingredients. Prices are very reasonable, and the menu includes charbroiled beef and chicken burgers as well as exotic dishes. Lively Hawaiian entertainment on Friday and Saturday night continues until 2:00 a.m.

A lively and more expensive restaurant, **Harrington's** (135 Kalanianaole Street, 961-4966), is situated in a romantic location overlooking Reed's Bay. Delicious food and atmosphere, music, and dancing, Tuesday through Saturday, will remind you more of San Francisco with a Hawaiian twist than of Hilo. For a change of nightlife scenery without a drastic change of atmosphere, try **Reflections Restaurant** (101 Aupini Street in the Hilo Lagoon Centre, 935-8501), a very classy and attractively decorated restaurant, and **Fiascos** (Waiakea Square, 200 Kanoelehua Avenue, on the way to the airport, 935-7666) on weekends for their excellent salad bar.

Cafe 100, 969 Kilauea Street, 935-8683, on your way out of town across from Kapiolani School, is a drive-in that belongs at the top of the lunch bargain list with its teriyaki steak, mahi mahi, chicken and steak dishes, and chili. Just follow the crowds of locals. Closed Sunday.

Dick's Coffee House, in the Hilo Shopping Center, 935-2769, at the corner of Kekuanaoa and Kilauea avenues, open 7:00 a.m. to 10:30 p.m., is unbeatable for variety and prices for all three meals, especially the specials, six days a week.

For breakfast, you can't beat **Ken's House of Pancakes**, 1730 Kamehameha Avenue, 935-8711, at the intersection of Kam Avenue and Banyan Drive. Open 24 hours, it offers pancakes all day, as well as burgers and classic roadside lunches and dinners from chicken to steak for under $8 and late-night eats and early "brunch" from midnight to 6:00 a.m.

Hilo is your best place on the Big Island and arguably in Hawaii for excellent Japanese cuisine and atmosphere at reasonable prices. **K.K. Tei Restaurant** (1550 Kam Highway, 961-3791) out toward the airport is a good example. **K.K. Place**, 413 Kilauea Avenue, 935-5216, has cafeteria-style breakfasts and Oriental and American plate lunches and dinners at budget prices. **Restaurant Fuji**, in the Hilo Hotel, 142 Kinoole Street, 961-3733, offers authentic and reasonably priced Japanese food, with outstanding hibachi-grilled food and a tempura bar, in comfortable indoor and outdoor settings. The Nihon Cultural Center's **Nihon Restaurant**, 123 Lihiwai St., 969-1133 (11:00 a.m.-2:00 p.m., 5:00-8:30 p.m.) has full-course dinners at moderate prices and also an excellent sushi bar. **Tom Zushi** (68 Mamo Street, 961-6100) wins the prize for inexpensive picnic fare, or two can dine sumptuously here for $15.

Ting-Hao Mandarin Restaurant (Puainako town center, off Highway 11 beyond the airport, 959-6288) serves every style of Chinese food, not just Mandarin. Chef Cheng's huge menu, the restaurant's low prices, generous portions, ample daily specials, variety of vegetarian dishes, and friendliness earn every hungry visitor's loyalty and gratitude. Presumably you won't be bothered by formica-topped tables and fluorescent lighting. This restaurant captures Hilo and the Big Island at its best. **Sun Sun Lau's Chop Sui House** (1055 Kinoole, 935-2808) is consistently selected as one of the Big Island's top Chinese restaurants, with amazingly reasonable gourmet food. **Leung's Chop Suey House** (530 East Lanikaula Street, 935-4066, at the intersection of Kanoelehua Avenue about a mile past Banyan Drive) is in an unappealing industrial area, but it serves some of the best eat-in or take-out Cantonese food in town, up to 8:30 p.m.

Roussel's, 60 Keawe Street (935-5000), is Hilo's best restaurant, a splurge serving tasty Louisiana Cajun/Creole dishes. Try the blackened fish.

Nightlife
Downtown Hilo shuts down by 9:00 p.m. Few bars stay open past 10:00 p.m. The hot spot for dancing is upstairs at **Apple Annie's**, 100 Kanoelehua Avenue. Rock 'n' rollers who don't want to dance should head for **J.D.'s Banyan Broiler** on Banyan Drive after 10:00 p.m. until 2:00 a.m. For a bar where you're likely to meet interesting locals, try **Rosey's Boathouse**. There's no place to dance, but an excellent guitar combo provides light background music for good conversation.

Much of Hilo's nightlife centers around the hotels. For a lively evening out, the **Springwater Cafe and Bar**, Waiakea Villas Hotel, has a light menu, drinks, and entertainment from pop to Hawaiian, Wednesday through Saturday until 2:00 a.m. The **Ho'omalimali Bar** of the Hawaii Naniloa Hotel has a disco that stays open on Friday and Saturday nights until 3:00 a.m.

Itinerary Options
Historic Downtown Hilo Walking Tour: A walking tour through the heart of historic Hilo covers a 24-block area with over 200 buildings of historical interest, including many in Pacific art deco style. The self-guided walking tour starts at Kalakaua Park, named in honor of King David Kalakaua. The first destination, across Kalakaua Street, is the Old Police Station, which houses the East Hawaii Cultural Center's Old Police Station Gallery.

Kalakaua Park, with a bronze statue of Hawaii's last king, is next to the Hilo Hotel; down Kalakaua Street, then right to Haili Street, with three (out of the original five) churches, down Kilauea Avenue, past the Taishoji Soto Mission started by Zen Buddhists (1913), to Furneaux Lane. Turn left on Kamehameha Avenue to see some interesting architecture: Renaissance Revival (Hafa Building); Mediterranean (the Vana Building); and even art deco (the S. H. Kress Building). Turn up Waianuenue Avenue to Keawe Street, and make a left to see several wooden buildings typical of early twentieth-century Hilo, which have been remodeled.

South of Hilo: Kauai may be the "Garden Isle," but over 2,500 species of plants and flowers flourish in the Big Island's landscape, 95 percent found only in Hawaii. At the eastern end of town on Highway 12, about two miles from the airport, **Hilo Tropical Gardens** (1477 Kalanianaole Avenue, 935-4957) display enough native Hawaiian shrubs, trees, tropical flowers, and other plants in its gardens to satisfy most visitors. Admission $1. You still need to see a nursery operation where tropical cut flowers, orchid sprays, and leis are packed for shipping. Drive south on Highway 11, take a right at Palai and a left on Kilauea Avenue to **Orchids of Hawaii** (2801 Kilauea Avenue). Admission free.

A few miles south of Hilo, across Highway 11 from Nani Mau Gardens, **Panaewa Rainforest Zoo** is a rare zoo featuring rain forest creatures in a natural setting. Open daily, 9:00 a.m. to 4:30 p.m., 959-7224, admission free. Ten miles from Hilo along Route 11 and three miles to the left through macadamia nut orchards is the **Mauna Loa Macadamia Nut Factory** (966-8612). Visit the processing operation (C. Brewer & Co.) and, at the same time, munch on a handful of free samples. From Hilo, it's only about an hour and a half on Highway 11, the two-lane Belt Road, to Hawaii Volcanoes National Park through Keaau, Kurtistown, Mountain View, Glenwood, and Volcano. In Keaau, across from Keaau Town Center shopping area, **Keaau Natural Foods and Bakery**, one of the most complete on the island, adjoins **Tonya's** (966-8091), a very good, tiny (5 tables) vegetarian restaurant (11:00 a.m.-7:00 p.m., Mon.-Fri., closed on the week-end), specializing in vegetarian Mexican dishes and smoothies.

Saddle Road and Mauna Kea Summit Trail: Like the spectacular road to Hana on Maui, Saddle Road is not the driving nightmare that you've heard about, and driving it opens up incomparable vistas. Check your gas beforehand since there are no gas stations for 87 miles.

Past Rainbow Falls, Saddle Road splits off to the left in about two miles. Alternatively, most visitors simply turn inland at the **Route 200** sign off Highway 19 just north of Hilo. On the way up the mountain, you'll pass **Kaumana Caves**, a lava tube worth exploring. The caves contain a fern grotto. If you intend to explore the caves, bring a flashlight.

Saddle Road first passes through thick rain forest, then fern and *ohia lehua* forest until the 3,000-foot level when the landscape changes dramatically to a vast lava flow. Midway up from either the Kona or Hilo side is the turnoff for the **Mauna Kea Summit Road**, paved until the **Ellison Onizuka Center for International Astronomy** (329-3441) at the 9,200-foot level. From this base camp for scientists and astronomers, a gravel road winds across and up the steep mountain another 7 miles nearly to the 14,000-foot level.

At Mauna Kea's summit, location of the world's foremost collection of optical and infrared telescopes, the **W. M. Keck Observatory**'s instruments will be on line by the time you read this book. At that time, the road to the summit will be paved, too. The best way to see Mauna Kea's observatory complex, view a magnificent sunset (with visibility that could range for 100 miles), and see the clear night sky full of stars through a portable telescope is with Monte Wright's **Paradise Safaris** (322-2366, $80 per person) or **Waipio Valley Shuttle/Mauna Kea Summit Tours** (775-7121). A 5- to 6-hour customized van tour by the owners of Waipio Shuttle, they will pick you up and drop you off in the Honokaa-Waimea area.

Five miles west of the Mauna Kea Observatory Road (20 miles from Highway 190), at 6,500 feet in the midst of rolling grasslands, seven fully furnished cabins (with hot showers as well as cooking utensils) in **Mauna Kea State Park (Pohakuloa)** can be rented from the State Department of Natural Resources (961-7200).

Among the four **Hawaiian Eyes-Big Island Bicycle Tours** (P.O. Box 1500, Honokaa, HI 96727, 885-8806), as of this writing, **Mauna Kea Iki** makes a 2½ hour ten-mile descent down a 3,000-foot slope of Mauna Kea ($48). A Saddle Road trip covers 27 miles and a 4,000-foot descent from 9:00 a.m. to 3:00 p.m. (including lunch, $90).

It's about a two-hour drive from Hilo's tropical nurseries to the frigid lunar landscapes of Mauna Kea and Mauna Loa where the endangered silversword plant and the nene goose, the state bird, thrive in rarified isolation. Waimea is 55 miles from Hilo via Saddle Road, descending 3,000 feet in 15 miles from Saddle Road through the gamebird grasslands of the Pohakuloa Area of Mauna Kea State Park. Kailua is 87 miles from Hilo on Saddle Road, a 2- to 3-hour drive if you're in a hurry.

You can drive to the 9,400-foot level of Mauna Kea in an ordinary passenger car, though car rental agencies will refuse to rent if you say that you're going to drive on the rough Saddle Road. Twenty-seven miles from Hilo, a 9-mile spur road leads to the Mauna Kea trailhead at Kilohana (9,620 feet) and a 17-mile road up Mauna Loa. At Humuula Junction, the **Mauna Kea Road** heads north and the **Mauna Loa Road** south. On the Mauna Loa Road, if your car is tuned for high altitudes you can drive 8 miles to a locked chain across the road (weekdays), 9 miles below the observatory, or the full 17 miles on weekends past fantastic black, silvery, brown, and reddish lava shapes. If you intend to get out of your car and walk around at altitudes above 4,000 feet, bring one or two layers of warm clothing (sweaters, jackets, or pullovers). At higher altitudes, temperatures can change suddenly to the 40s Fahrenheit and near freezing at the summits.

At the 12,000-foot level, a trail leads a quarter mile from the jeep road to the **Keanakakoi** (Cave of the Adzes), where ancient Hawaiians mined stones for their adzes. Almost at the top is **Lake Waiau** (13,020 feet), the highest lake in the United States, 400 feet across and 15 feet down to an impervious bottom in a porous mountain.

THE BIG ISLAND: HAMAKUA COAST TO WAIPIO VALLEY

Drive on Highway 19 along the northeast coast and stop at one of the most beautiful botanical gardens in the Hawaiian Islands. Cross deep jungle canyons in Mauna Kea's slope and drive up the steep road to Akaka Falls at Honomu. Drive along Pepeekeo Scenic Drive, then glimpse old Hawaii as you pass by tiny tin-roofed and weather-beaten plantation towns with picturesque churches to Honokaa, the macadamia nut capital of the world. Turn onto Highway 24 to the lookout over Waipio Valley. You can hike down into the valley or take a four-wheel-drive or mule tour.

Suggested Schedule

7:00 a.m.	Breakfast in Hilo and checkout.
8:00 a.m.	Stop at Suisan Fish Market.
9:00 a.m.	Visit Hawaii Tropical Botanical Garden.
10:30 a.m.	Leave for Akaka Falls along the scenic drive to Onomea Bay.
11:00 a.m.	Akaka Falls State Park.
12:30 p.m.	Lunch in Honokaa, then visit the Kamaaina Woods shop and possibly the Hawaiian Holiday Macadamia Nut Factory.
1:30 p.m.	Leave Honokaa for the Waipio Valley Lookout and to explore fabulous Waipio Valley.
1:45 p.m.	Visit the Waipio Woodworks in Kukuihaele.
2:30 p.m.	Waipio Valley Lookout.
3:00 p.m.	Descend to Waipio Valley.
7:00 p.m.	Dinner and early to bed in Waipio Valley at the Waipio Hotel, or drive to Kukuihaele, Honokaa, or Kamuela.

Driving Route

The drive from Hilo to Honokaa, on a wide, smooth highway following Mauna Kea's northeastern slope, is only 39 miles. Follow Route 19 and the Mamalahoa Highway, the parallel old scenic road northeast from Hilo up the rain-swept Hamakua coast, a gently rolling plateau covered with sugarcane fields ending in cliffs over the sea, dotted with tiny plantation towns like Laupahoehoe, Papaaloa, Paauilo, and Paauhau. Drive on the 4-mile Pepeekeo Scenic Drive across wooden bridges along Onomea Bay. Turn inland on Route 220 past the Honomu Plantation Store to beautiful Akaka Falls. Don't expect to find any resorts (yet) on the Hamakua Coast, only very quiet villages holding onto portions of the old highway replaced by Highway 19. From Honokaa, a paved road, Highway 24, runs 10 miles (through—actually past—Kukuihaele) to the lookout over Waipio Valley's east rim.

Sightseeing Highlights
▲**Suisan Fish Market**—Stop in Hilo at 85 Lihiwai Street to see shop owners bidding in many languages for the day's fish catch. Arrive by 8:00 a.m. when the bidding starts.

▲▲▲**Hawaii Tropical Botanical Garden**—Five miles north of Hilo near the start of the 4-mile scenic road along Onomea Bay, this garden consists of 27 acres running the gamut of Hawaii's flora, with waterfalls, streams, and a lily pond. Bring mosquito repellent to fully enjoy the botanical environment.

Visitors are taken down to the valley in a shuttle van from the HTBG's parking lot and registration area about half a mile from the garden's entrance along Turtle Bay and 1 mile from the turnoff on Route 19 which says Scenic Route 4 Miles Long. The last minibus departs for the garden at 4:30 p.m. Adults are charged a $12 tax-deductible admission fee, and children under 16 are admitted free.

▲Drive 10 miles north of Hilo on Highway 19 to the turnoff on your left for Route 220 to **Honomu**. The **Honomu Plantation Store** is worth a visit just to see photographs of plantation life along the Hamakua Coast at the turn of the century. You can buy some snack items for a picnic, coffee, and delicious pastry at the bakery next door.

▲▲▲**Hilo to Honokaa**—Follow Route 220 past sugarcane fields for another 3 miles to Akaka Falls State Park. Besides several stunning falls, the 65-acre park in the junglelike gulch contains tropical plants from all over the world.

The stream from Akaka Falls runs 4 miles toward the ocean and empties at Kolekole Beach Park under the first bridge on Highway 19 north of Honomu, a popular local picnic area with camping facilities (county permit required). A much better spot for picnics or just a rest stop is Laupahoehoe Point, a beautiful peninsula just 11 miles from Honakaa. Papa'Aloa, just south of Laupahoehoe, is a picturesque village thick with tropical growth and palm trees.

One of the least visited natural areas on the Big Island, 100-acre Kalopa State Park is easily accessible, 2 miles south of Honokaa and another 2 miles up a good secondary road. The park provides a rare opportunity to explore one or more of the lush gulches along the Hamakua Coast. Best of all, in addition to tent camping with a state permit, several cabins are available (call 961-7200). A series of well-marked nature trails identify a tremendous variety of flora. Walk through groves of acacia, koa, kopiko, pilo and hapuu along the Native Forest Nature Trail.

▲**Honokaa**—Forty miles north of Hilo on Highway 240, Honokaa is the second-largest city on the Big Island. Honokaa only has 2,500 residents, and it still feels like the 1920s. However, a real estate and population boom is in the making as the Hamakua Sugar Company seeks solvency by selling off a large part of its holdings for development. Main street Honokaa consists of false-front buildings and local stores with a smattering of shops catering to tourists. One of the Big Island's and the world's largest macadamia nut growing areas, Honokaa is 9 miles from Waipio Valley and 16 miles from Waimea. From the center of town, take Lehua Street down a steep hill toward the sea to the Hawaiian Holiday Macadamia Nut Factory, open daily 9:00 a.m. to 6:00 p.m. The macadamia nut industry in Hawaii, currently another depressed agricultural business, actually started in Honokaa. On the way down the hill is

Kamaiina Woods, a factory and gift shop (with an outlet in
Waimea's Opelo Plaza) for handcrafted items from koa,
milo, and other local woods. Open daily 10:00 a.m. to 5:00
p.m.

▲▲▲**Waipio Valley**—At the Waipio Valley Lookout (at
the end of Route 24 just beyond Kukuihaele), a ribbon of
sparkling white surf disappears around the headland in
the corner of your eye as you gaze down on Waipio
Valley. A mile wide at the sea, it is six miles deep in rich
green, checkered with taro patches, bounded by 2,000-
foot-high cliffs, and constantly watered from the pali at the
rear of the valley. Hawaii's highest waterfall, Hiilawe
Waterfall, cascades 1,300 feet to the valley floor.
Kamehameha the Great came many times to the valley,
where many great kings were buried, to renew his spiritual power.

You can hike down to the valley, or let Les Baker and
the Waipio Valley Shuttle's Land Rover, 775-7121, drive
you down from the lookout (10 miles from Honokaa), 900
feet above the pali coast. The round-trip cost is $40 for
adults, $20 for children, for an hour-and-a-half tour or $60
to $100 for a half- to a full-day jeep and hiking tour into
the valley, including a light lunch. This same company
offers the state-authorized four-wheel-drive tour of Mauna
Kea, a 6-hour trip for $65 per person. An alternative to
Rovers and Jeeps is provided by Peter Tobin: Waipio
Valley Wagon Tours is a 2-hour trip by mule wagon,
Wednesday through Monday, for $45 per person (half
price for children under 12). Call 775-9518 for reservations.

Where to Stay

As the next best thing to camping, for $15 per person per
night you can stay at octogenarian taro farmer Tom Araki's
five-room **Waipio Hotel** (no water, electricity, or refrigera-
tor, two kitchens equipped with Coleman stoves and
kerosene lamps), with reservations (no deposits) arranged
by mail at least a month in advance to Tom Araki, 25
Malana Place, Hilo, HI 96720, or contact Waipio Valley
Shuttle, or call 775-0368 or 935-7466 (Hilo). Bring your
own food from the Last Chance Store next to the shuttle's

office. It's 2 miles from the lookout to the hotel in the valley. Bring plenty of mosquito repellent for the hike or ride. The nearby river has fresh prawns, and the road to the beach is lined with fruit trees.

Waipio Wayside (P.O. Box 840, Honokaa, HI 96727, 775-0275 or toll-free 800-833-8849), Jacqueline Horne's renovated and very charming sugar plantation home, is bordered by a white picket fence that is unmistakable from the road. This lovely retreat has five tastefully redecorated rooms for rent—from one with shared bath at $55 to the Bird's-Eye Room, a $85 suite opening onto the deck and garden.

The **Hamakua Hideaway**, Box 5104, Kukuihaele, HI 96727, 775-7425 (3 houses down from the Waipio Woodworks) is a B&B, less than one mile from the Waipio Lookout, at $60 per night. Christan Hunt's two units—the treehouse suite, nestled in a huge 100-year-old mango tree ($60 per night or $350 per week), and the cliff house (with fireplace, $75 per night, lower rates for a longer stay), on a cliff overlooking Maui, are rustic, secluded, and an excellent value. Guided jeep trips leave from in front of the Woodworks a few doors away.

At the 2,500-foot elevation on Mauna Kea, in Ahualoa 3 miles from Honoka toward Kamuela, the rustic **Log House B&B Inn** (P.O. Box 1495, Honokaa, HI 96727, 775-9990) has 5 nicely furnished bedrooms, 2 with private baths, a living room with fireplace and a library upstairs, all for $55 with an excellent breakfast. To get to the Log House, turn left at Tex Drive-In and then right on Mamalahoa Highway. Mamalahoa Highway winds up the mountainside 11 miles through Ahualoa to rejoin Highway 19, about 6 miles from Waimea Center, after crossing beautiful rolling pastureland. In Ahualoa, off twisting tree-lined roads to hidden-away places, where usually no one drives unless they know someone living there, is another of the Big Island's finest B&Bs: Michael Cowan's **Mountain Meadow Ranch B&B** (775-9376, $55 per couple), with 2 lovely bedrooms for rent on the private first floor, with their own sauna and bathroom, and a patio leading to a pretty garden in the woods.

For those who opt not to stay in Waipio Valley but to head for Waimea, very pleasant rooms are available at **Kamuela Inn** (P.O. Box 1004, Kamuela, HI 96743, Route 19, 885-4243, $55 to $79 single or double), with free (but skimpy) continental breakfast. The 19 rooms all have private baths, refrigerators, and cable TV. The newer, very attractively decorated and furnished **Parker Ranch Lodge** (P.O. Box 458, Kamuela, HI 96743, Route 19, 885-4100, $75-$85), is also within walking distance of the center of sightseeing, shopping, and eating. The 10 units have king or double beds, shower/ tubs, telephones, and TV.

Where to Eat

On the way up to Akaka Falls, **Ishigo's Inn and General Store**, 963-6128, in Honomu Village, has munchies and a remodeled B&B. The **Hotel Honokaa Club & Restaurant**, Route 24, 775-0678, serves a mix of Japanese and American food, breakfast, lunch, and excellent seafood and steak dinners at moderate prices. Otherwise, drive to Kamuela for the best dinner choices (see Day 13).

Itinerary Options

Waimanu Valley is for the adventuresome with hiking experience and stamina. Continue from Waipio Valley for nine miles on the Waimanu Valley Trail. The trail climbs up steep cliffs to the adjoining and even wilder valley, through a series of fourteen gulches. The trail shelter is nine gulches from Waipio Valley, two-thirds of the way to Waimanu. About half the size of Waipio Valley, Waimanu is very similar. Waiilikahi Falls is about 1½ miles along the northwest pali of the valley, and the large pool of water for swimming below it is worth making your own trail there. There's water in the valley (boil or treat it, though) and numerous beachfront campsites, or you can return that night to Waipio.

Waipio Ranch, operated by Sherri Hannum and Wayne Teves, has horseback rides into Waipio Valley which can be arranged 24 hours in advance through Joe Matthieu at Waipio Woodworks, 775-0958. A half-day tour costs $55, full-day $100, including a four-wheel-drive ride down and back up the valley to Kukuihaele.

THE BIG ISLAND: KAMUELA AND NORTH KOHALA

On the way from Waipio to the base of the mountainous Kohala peninsula, travel through a temperate zone of green meadows and darker green trees to Kamuela, a thriving town with at least 50 new stores and restaurants in several shopping centers, several of the best restaurants on the islands, a performing arts theater, and other delightful surprises.

Suggested Schedule	
6:00 a.m.	If you have the energy, rise early to catch the sunrise at Waipio Valley's black sand beach. (If you stayed over in the Honokaa area or Kamuela, you can sleep in.)
8:00 a.m.	If you're not hiking from Waipio Valley to Waimanu, after breakfast return to Route 24 for the drive to Kamuela and check in. (Hikers to Waimanu, come to Kamuela tonight.)
10:00 a.m.	Visit to the Parker Ranch Visitor Center and Museum, followed by local shopping.
12:00 noon	Lunch in Kamuela.
1:30 p.m.	Leave for North Kohala's Hawi, Kapaau, and Pololu—driving on beautiful Highway 250.
2:30 p.m.	Arrive in Hawi.
3:00 p.m.	Browsing in Hawi and Kapaau.
3:30 p.m.	Drive to the Pololu Valley Lookout and walk down to the beach. Option: Visit Mookini Luakini Heiau, Kamehameha's birthplace and/or Lapakahi State Historical Park before returning to Kamuela.
6:00 p.m.	Backtrack to Kamuela or North Kohala for dinner.
7:00 p.m.	Dinner, a moonlight stroll, and overnight in Kamuela or Kohala resorts.

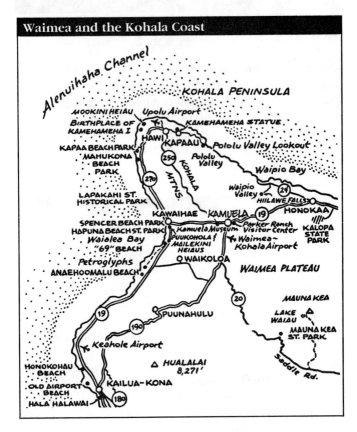

Waimea and the Kohala Coast

Kamuela offers the best of both worlds as touring base: great hiking or horseback riding in the cooler mountains, some of Hawaii's most beautiful beaches only minutes away, and relatively low-priced accommodations. Leaving Kamuela, drive the 20 miles of Highway 250 between Kamuela and Hawi to visit a black sand beach, Kamehameha's birthplace and the sacrificial temple, Mookini Luakini Heiau.

Sightseeing Highlights

▲**Parker Ranch Visitor Center and Museum**, Highway 19, Kamuela, 885-7655—A frustrated and adventuresome sailor from Newton, Massachusetts, John Parker Palmer, jumped ship in Hawaii in 1809 and created a dynasty that changed the history of the Big Island forever. With over 250,000 acres spreading across North Kona, South Kohala, Waimea, and North Kohala, Parker Ranch today is the largest cattle ranch in the United States, raising one of the largest Hereford herds in the world. Parker imported cowboys from Mexico and South America—*paniolos* (a Hawaiian version of *Españoles*)—to work as ranch hands.

The museum at Parker Ranch Visitor Center, first stop on a tour of the ranch, was started by Thelma Parker Smart, mother of the ranch's current owner, Richard Smart. It depicts the history and genealogy of six generations of Parker Ranch owners, displaying old family photos, furnishings, special and day-to-day clothing, old saddles and other riding paraphernalia, and other interesting items. One room is dedicated to Duke Kahanamoku, the Hawaiian Olympian and sheriff of Oahu for 25 years credited with introducing surfing to Australia.

Shuttle buses take visitors around the ranch to see Puukalani Stable and the adjoining horse-drawn carriage museum and two Parker family historic homes: Puuopelu and Mana.

The visitor's center and museum are open from 9:30 a.m. to 3:30 p.m. Admission $5 for adults, $3.75 for children. The two-hour Paniolo Shuttle Tour by mini-van to Puukalani Stables, the working ranch, and the historic homes at Puuopelu costs $15 for adults, $7.50 for children under 12. Another two hours and $39 for adults and $19 for children will take you on the Paniolo Country Tour to the original homestead site of Mana and the Parker family cemetery, with lunch included. Call 885-7655.

▲▲**The Kamuela Museum**, junction of Routes 19 and 250, 885-4724—Founded by descendants of John Palmer Parker, this museum is a collection of Royal Hawaiiana and artifacts from around the world, such as stuffed animals and reptiles from four continents, assorted ancient weaponry, pioneer clothing, and Chinese furnishings, as well as photographs of the Parker family through the years. Admission: $2.50 for adults, $1 for children under 12.

▲▲▲**North Kohala**—This was the home of Kameha-meha the Great, from which he launched a conquest of all the islands. The shores of this peninsula contain many historical sites. At the end of coastal Route 270 (Akoni Pule Highway), which passes through Hawi and Kapaau, is the steep pali overlooking Pololu Valley, a major taro valley of old Hawaii, accessible by a trail from the lookout.

▲▲**Route 250 (Kohala Mountain Road)**—Winding through the Kohala Mountains, this very scenic route reaches an elevation of 3,500 feet. With views of the shimmering peaks of Mauna Kea, Mauna Loa, and Hualalai and the plains and ocean below, Route 250 is a memorable drive from Highway 19 near Kamuela to Hawi at the northern tip of the peninsula. All along this winding road, a succession of spectacular views frame the western shoreline.

Riding in the Kohala Mountains with Ironwood Outfitters, located next to Kohala Ranch, opens up views of the ocean, pastures, and mountains that are unsurpassed on the Big Island.

▲**Hawi**, a former plantation town and the Big Island's northernmost town, is full of rustic and derelict charm. Before the Kohala Sugar Company pulled out in the early 1970s, the town could boast of four movie the-aters. Today there are none. Colorful old houses and false-front stores in Hawi also resemble Makawao and Paia on Maui, or a bustling version of Kauai's compar-atively quiet Hanapepe. The King's Trail Inn (889-5606), formerly the Old Hawaii Lodging Company (and previous to that, Luke's Hotel), and a large restaurant-entertainment spot next door, Hale Alii (889-0206), in the center of town are visible signs of change. In con-trast, catering mainly to local people, the Kohala Club Hotel (889-6793) in Kapaau has not changed much in fifty years (and apparently doesn't care). Along the road to the Pololu Valley Lookout stands the original gilt and bronze statue of Kamehameha the Great. (The statue of Kamehameha in downtown Honolulu is a replica.)

▲▲From **Pololu Valley Lookout**, the valley floor and a black sand beach are visible 300 feet below. Looking down the fantastic coastline of Hawaii's pali of hidden valleys, gorges, and luxurious foliage, you see the only access to the shoreline is a dirt trail down to Pololu Beach. Pololu is five valleys and 12 miles from Waipio Valley. The trail down to Pololu is an easy 15-minute walk past thick lauhala growth.

Where to Stay

Upcountry Hideaways consists of three B&B cottages, each in a beautiful location, with a different decor, and very hospitable and knowledgeable hosts: Doug and Dodi MacArthur's modern **Puu Manu Cottage** (885-6247, $85), a two-bedroom cottage in a pasture on the "wet side" of Kamuela, with beautiful views of Mauna Kea; Barbara and Charlie Campbell's **Waimea Gardens Cottage** (885-4550, $85) in natural wood, with antique furnishings, located on the "dry side" of Kamuela, near a stream flowing down from the Kohala Mountains in the background; and at the beginning of Highway 250 to Hawi, **Hawaii Country Cottage** (885-7441, $65), with a completely private bedroom, living room, bathroom, and kitchen. All of these B&Bs and many more on the Big Island and throughout Hawaii can be reserved through Barbara Campbell's **Hawaii's Best Bed & Breakfasts** (P.O. Box 563, Kamuela, HI 96743, 885-4550 or toll-free 800-262-9912).

Where to Eat

It is really a pity to plan an itinerary that doesn't include lunch or dinner in Kamuela. Even the **delicatessen** in Parker Ranch Shopping Center's Sure Save Supermarket is one of the best places in Hawaii to put together the ingredients of picnic lunches and a good enough reason to make Kamuela your base for touring the northern part of the Big Island. Except for genuine bagels, even New Yorkers will not miss Manhattan's best delis.

The Bread Depot (885-6354) in the Opelo Plaza on Kawaihae Road is a delightful bakery-deli for daily specials (Italian, Greek, who knows?), huge, warm cinnamon buns, good (but not excellent) French bread, tasty soups, salads, desserts, and average coffee with free refills. Open 6:30 a.m. to 5:30 p.m. except Sunday. Two of Kamuela's restaurants are among the best in Hawaii: Peter Merriman's **Merriman's** (885-6822) and, across the road, Hans Peter Hager's **Edelweiss** (885-6800, no reservations). Former chef at the Mauna Lani Bay hotel, Chef Merriman has set a standard for Pacific Rim cuisine on the island using locally grown produce, beef, and herbs to create one of the island's finest and most interesting menus.

Aloha Luigi's (885-7277), near the intersection of Routes 19 and 190, uses all the local herbs that Chef Luigi can get his hands on for delicious pestos and other sauces. Luigi's deserves its rave reviews from visiting diners for pastas and pizzas served at reasonable prices.

Really good breakfasts are hard to find in Kamuela. The **Waimea Coffee Shop** across the street from Gallery of Great Things has the best cup of coffee in town and some decent pastries ("imported" from the French Bakery on Kaiwe Street in Kailua-Kona). Otherwise, for hearty breakfasts, join the locals at **Massayo's** in the Hayashi Building near the Kamuela Inn or at **Auntie Alice's Restaurant and Bakery** in the Parker Ranch Shopping Center.

Great Wall Chopsui (885-7252) has moved to the Waimea Center where it continues to serve tasty, inexpensive Chinese food. Besides offering patrons a red velvet saloon, the fanciest bar in Waimea, Chef Al Salvador specializes in cuts of Parker Ranch beef in any form, including paniolo stew, at the **Parker Ranch Broiler** (885-7366). Victorian decor for booths and tables gives the restaurant a classy cowboy-country feeling. Another beef emporium that you can count on for delicious and huge portions is **Cattleman's Steakhouse** (885-4077), adjoining the Waimea Center. Both the Broiler and the Steakhouse are the only places to look for evening entertainment in Kamuela on weekends.

Nightlife

The ranch's **Kahilu Theater** (885-6017) across from the Parker Ranch Visitor Center brings about a dozen top theatrical, dance, and concert events to Kamuela each season. The current owner of the ranch, Richard Smart, great-great-great-grandson of the founder, is a thespian and responsible for bringing theater and performing arts to Kamuela which outshine most towns of similar size elsewhere in the United States.

Itinerary Options

En route to the birthplace and home of Kamehameha, the shoreline of North Kohala is etched with historical sites and beach parks that tourists rarely visit.

Lapakahi State Historical Park (A.D 1300), a 600-year-old, partially restored Hawaiian fishing village, stands on isolated, rugged terrain about 12 miles from Kawaihae. Open daily for self-guided and guided tours, canoe sheds, a fishing shrine, a demonstration of Hawaiian salt-making, exhibits of games (that children of all ages are encouraged to try), numerous house sites, stone tools and utensils, and other interesting artifacts are displayed along trails around the site. From December through April, you may even see migrating whales near shore.

Originally built for human sacrifices, the remains of 20-foot stone walls surrounding **Mookini Heiau National Historic Site** are reached by a left turn on a bumpy unpaved road at the end of Upolu Airfield's runway. (After a heavy rain, this road requires a four-wheel drive.) Surf pounds against steep cliffs below windswept fields around this sacred site, home of all-powerful gods, once the exclusive domain of *alii* who came to worship here as early as the twelfth century. The remaining foundation is an irregular triangle measuring 125 by 250 feet, with 30-foot-high and 15-foot-thick walls. Offerings (not human, of course) are still to be seen on the altar.

The heiau is only a few hundred yards from Kamehameha's birthplace—**Kamehameha Akahi Aina Hanau**. Inside the low stone wall around this historic place are some boulders believed to be the actual stones on which Kamehameha, unifier of the Hawaiian kingdom, was born around 1752.

THE BIG ISLAND: SOUTH KOHALA AND KONA COAST

Stop for lunch at one of Hawaii's best and most beautiful swimming beaches, Spencer Beach, with visits to at least two more white sand gems on the way south to Kailua-Kona. The resorts of the South Kohala and North Kona Coast, among the finest and most diverse in Hawaii, deserve a visit for sightseeing on the grounds, lunch or dinner, or picnicking on their beaches, all open to the public.

Suggested Schedule

8:00 a.m.	After a leisurely breakfast, leave Kamuela for Pu'ukohola Heiau National Historic Site, then south to Kawaihae Bay and the start of South Kohala's coastal attractions and beaches.
10:00 a.m.	Visit Pu'ukohola and Mailekini Heiau.
12:00 noon	Leisurely picnic lunch on Spencer Beach or try Mauna Kea's famous buffet lunch.
1:30 p.m.	Hapuna Beach for swimming, strolling, or relaxing.
2:30 p.m.	See the Puako petroglyphs.
3:30 p.m.	Swim or snorkel at Anaehoomalu Bay.
5:00 p.m.	Drive to Kailua-Kona and check in.
7:00 p.m.	Sunset dining and then strolling near Kailua Wharf and the Hotel King Kamehameha.

Sightseeing Highlights

▲▲▲**South Kohala Coast**—This coast north of Kailua-Kona has some of the best swimming beaches anywhere in the islands: Spencer Beach Park near Kawaihae and just below the Pu'ukohola Heiau, Hapuna Beach (one of the finest white sand beaches in the hemisphere), Anaehoomalu Beach fronting on the Royal Waikoloan Hotel (one of the most beautiful), and Kaun'oa Beach, which fronts on the Westin Mauna Kea Hotel. All of these beaches have public access.

▲▲Pu'ukohola and the Mailekini Heiau—One mile south of Kawaihae, where Route 270 turns into Route 19, is a National Historic Site (Pu'ukohola) preserving Mailekini Heiau and the John Young House. Mailekini Heiau is the last major temple built on the Big Island. Kamehameha built this sacrificial temple in 1791 for his war god, Ku, after a prophet told him to conquer all of Hawaii. When it was completed, he invited his chief rival, Keoua Kuahuula, to the dedication and slew him before he reached shore. In the next 4 years he conquered all the islands except Kauai. John Young, an English seaman who became Kamehameha's close adviser, taught Hawaiians how to use cannon and musket, converted Mailekini Heiau into a fort, and became a Hawaiian chief.

▲▲King's Trail—Invisible along the coastline is a trail—the Ala Kahakai—of smooth rocks built by ancient Hawaiians to ease the trip across the island over rough lava. Later, cattle were run on the trail to docks at Kawaihae, and donkey caravans carried salt to and from Kailua. The King's Trail passes along the edge of Kona Village Resort—past ponds, tide pools, and lava tubes filled with clear water, and Loretta Lynn's house and other private estates at Kiholo Bay—and inconspicuously hugs the coastline past all North Kona and South Kohala coastal resorts.

▲▲The Mauna Kea Beach Hotel—The hotel's collection of more than 1,500 art treasures from the Pacific and Asia is a museum in a beautiful resort set in 500 manicured acres. For a hotel that is as expensive and exclusive as the Mauna Kea, its rooms are surprisingly simple in decor and furnishings. Art tours are conducted twice a week for guests and others.

▲▲Beaches of Puako and Hapuna—"69" Beach (Waialea Bay) is named for a marker on the main highway near Hapuna Beach Park. Turn down to Hapuna Beach Park, pass the entrance to the park, and stay on the paved road that passes the turnoff to the park. In a little more than a half mile, turn on the dirt road to the right and take the left fork down the hill to the beach. The same road can be reached by taking a left from Highway 19 at the Puako turnoff and then the next right to reach the dirt road turnoff (to the left this time) described above. Between Hapuna and the Mauna Lani Resort, Puako is a residential community along three miles of Puako Bay.

Tide pools and snorkeling along this coast are excellent. Deservedly crowded on weekends, Hapuna Beach State Park is one of the nicest beaches in Hawaii. Only three miles from Kawaihae, this wide white sand beach is bordered by kiawe, hala, and coconut trees (now surrounded by Mauna Kea resort development). Above the beach, six very basic screened A-frame shelters sleeping four people each can be rented for a nominal fee from the Division of State Parks.

▲▲**Mauna Lani Bay Resort**—The resort is set in a historic area known as Kalahuipua, along the King's Trail, where Kamehameha I built a small village and canoe landing at Keawanui Bay.

In addition to its fantastic golf courses, the pristine white sand beach on a lovely cove below the six-story structure, historic fish ponds in a beautifully landscaped area, 10 tennis courts in a garden pavilion, and other amenities make this one of the top resorts in the world. With these attractions, the Mauna Lani can rent two-bedroom oceanside "bungalows" with their own swimming pool and jacuzzi for $2,000 a night (including a chauffeured limousine, a butler around the clock, and a maid on call). Luxurious 2- and 3-bedroom condominiums at Mauna Lani Terrace (800-882-4252) and Mauna Lani Point (800-642-6284) are run like a self-contained hotel, with all of the services of the hotel. Mauna Lani Bay Resort now includes the 542-room Ritz Carlton-Mauna Lani Bay (800-241-3333) that, in addition to elegant public areas, plush rooms, and beautifully landscaped courtyards, adds three more restaurants to the wealth of previously existing restaurants at the resort.

▲▲**Puako Petroglyphs**—Ordinary people, not artists, seem to have made the linear and triangular figures—warriors, canoes, paddles, spears, and other objects. The drawings were made as part of ritual or prayer, and speak of spiritual phenomena—*mana*.

Waikoloa—At mile marker 74 on Highway 19, look for Waikoloa Road weaving up Mauna Kea's lower slopes for

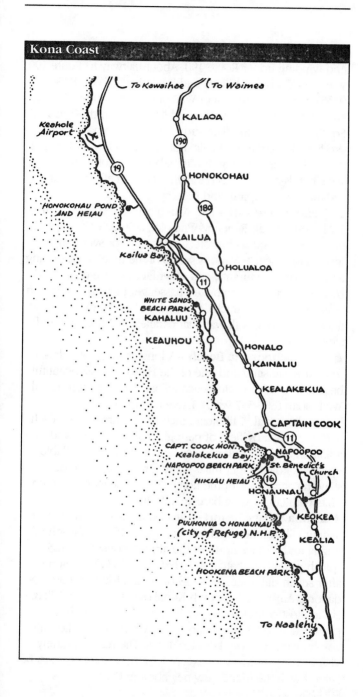

13 miles, connecting coastal Route 19 with the more scenic and winding upper Route 190. About halfway to Route 190, you pass Waikoloa Village and Waikoloa Stables (883-9335). Short-term rentals in Waikoloa Villas (800-367-7042) would put you closer to the middle of the North Kona and South Kohala resorts. The sunshine in Waikoloa is more predictable than in Kamuela, but Waikoloa is windier. In a choice between staying in Kamuela or Waikoloa, Kamuela wins hands-down for economy rentals, excellent B&Bs, restaurants, shopping, and scenery.

▲**Waikoloan Resort**—The Waikoloan Resort features the 1,241-room Hyatt Regency Waikoloa (800-223-1234) on 62 acres landscaped with protected lagoons for swimming instead of a beach. Various wings of the hotel, its shopping areas, seven restaurants, and other facilities are connected by a monorail and motorized passenger boats operating on parallel canals and tracks. Oriental art fills the grounds and lines a mile-long walkway that parallels the monorail and canal route.

▲▲▲**Anaehoomalu Beach**—A long crescent of palm-fringed white sand and one of the Hawaii's most beautiful beaches, Anaehoomalu Beach adjoins the 543-room Royal Waikoloan (800-537-9800). Drive into the resort and, just before the Royal Waikoloan, make a left turn to the beach and also a nearby field of petroglyphs. This beach and two adjoining 18-hole golf courses (and a third one available up in Waikoloa, eight miles away) are some of the outstanding attractions of the hotel. With these assets, garden units with lanais are a bargain at $110.

▲▲**Kona Village Resort**—Built on the site of an ancient fishing village, the Kona Village Resort, 15 miles north of Kailua and 7 miles north of the airport, consists of 125 "plush primitive" thatched-roofed huts (*hales*), fashioned after seven different styles of Polynesian island accommodations. Among all of South Kohala's resorts, Kona Village is the most complete escape from reality. All meals are provided. The hales contain no television sets, radios, air-conditioners, or even keys for doors. The resort is barely visible from Highway 19 except for a new golf course to be shared with the brand new neighboring Four Seasons

Hotel, another oasis speck on the ocean surrounded by black volcanic rumble.

Where to Stay

South Kohala: About 30 miles before you get to Kailua-Kona, the 38 one- to three-bedroom units of the **Puako Beach Condominiums**, 3 Puako Beach Drive, Puako, 882-7711, start at $80 per night and will put you near Spencer, Hapuna, and Anaehoomalu beaches.

Kailua-Kona and Keauhou: The **Hotel King Kamehameha**, 75-5660 Palani Road, 329-2911 or 800-227-4700, has nicely decorated rooms, all with great views of the bay from lanais, starting at $85 per person. The **Kona Tiki Hotel**, Alii Drive, 329-1425, has 17 refurbished units, with ceiling fans, refrigerators, some kitchenettes, and lanais for about $70 with a three-day minimum, in a garden setting with a pool by the sea, a mile south of Kailua-Kona. With spacious rooms, lanais, in-room refrigerators, beautiful grounds, pool and saltwater swimming, on its own peninsula, the 535 rooms at the **Kona Surf Resort** (78-128 Ehukai St., Kailua-Kona, HI 96740, 800-367-8011 or 322-3411) are an excellent value at $99 to $155. One-bedrooms at $135 for up to four people and two-bedroom condominium units at **Kanaloa at Keauhou** (78-261 Manukai, 322-2272, Colony Hotels & Resorts, 32 Merchant Street, Honolulu HI 96813, 800-657-7872) are a good buy. These 37 low-rise buildings on 17 acres with three pools, tennis courts, and nicely landscaped grounds contain spacious, elegant rooms with big shower-bath-jacuzzis and full kitchens.

Sea Village has spacious, beautifully furnished apartments, kitchens with modern appliances, and ultra-nice bathrooms, with one-bedroom garden view units at $80 to oceanview at $110 going up another $20 in high season (Sea Village Condominium Resort, c/o Paradise Management Corporation, Kukui Plaza C-207, 50 S. Beretania St., Hon. HI 96813, 800-367-5205 or 538-7145). Continue south on Highway 11 to Honalo, about seven miles from Kailua-Kona, where at 1,300 feet above sea level you have two very different low-budget choices: the very charming, Japanese-style retreat at **Teshima's Inn**, 322-9140, $30 single and $35 double.

The 4-story **Uncle Billy's Kona Bay Hotel**, 75-5739 Alii Drive, Kailua-Kona, HI 96740, 935-7903, with pool, restaurant, and bar situated in the middle, has nicely furnished, large rooms with mini-kitchenettes and an appealing and relaxing atmosphere. It qualifies as inexpensive to moderate, $72 to $79 single or double with car and breakfast.

Holualoa: The **Holualoa Inn** (P.O. Box 222, Holualoa, HI, 96725, 324-1121) on 40 acres of pastureland, coffee groves, and lush growth has four lovely guest rooms, each with a different theme and decor for $100 to $200, with choices of king, queen, and twin beds, shared and private bathrooms. Goro and Yayoko Inaba's more than 60-year-old **Kona Hotel** (Mamalahoa Highway, Holualoa, HI 96725, 324-1155) has 11 clean and airy rooms, the best accommodations bargain on the Big Island at $23 per night for two, $15 for one person.

Where to Eat

On the second level of the Kawaihae Shopping Center, **Harrington's** (882-7997) restaurant, a branch of Harrington's in Hilo, serves everything from prime ribs to calimari in stylish surroundings. On the first level, **Cafe Pesto** (882-1071) serves some of the best pasta, pesto, and pizza on the Big Island. Nearby on Route 27, the garden terrace at the **Blue Dolphin Family Style Restaurant** (882-7771) is a pleasant place to eat light fare. Very local and relaxed, noisy, smoky, and fun, **The Polihali Bar** (882-7076) in the Kawaihae Shopping Center is one of the few places to dance north of Kohala resorts.

At the Hyatt Regency Waikoloa's **Donatoni's**, where you pay for the best northern Italian food, service, and ambience, and you get it. The same is true for Japanese food at the **Imari** and French continental cuisine at the **Water's Edge** (885-1234). The Royal Waikoloan has several adequate restaurants: the **Garden Cafe**, a moderate-priced open-air coffee shop and the **Tiara Room** serving French-Polynesian cuisine in a wood-paneled room at deluxe prices. Dining and dancing are combined nicely at the

Royal Terrace.

A gastronomical tour of the Mauna Lani Bay Resort now includes the Ritz Carlton-Mauna Lani Bay's Chef Padovani's **Cafe and Ocean Bar and Grill** and the more formal **The Grill** and **The Dining Room** (800-241-3333 or 885-0099); and five excellent Mauna Lani restaurants—**Le Soleil** with a distinguished French menu, the partially open **Bay Terrace**, Chef Alan Wong's gourmet Pacific Rim cuisine at the **Canoe House**, Chef Ann Sutherland's superbly creative meat to seafood dishes at the **Gallery** (885-7777) and continental cuisine with an emphasis on seafood at the **Third Floor** (885-6622).

Chef Glen Alos at **The Kona Village** (325-5555) presides over one of the finest "Pacific Rim" menus on the Big Island but outdoes himself at the hotel's luau with a buffet that is unsurpassed for variety and quality in Hawaii, combining Hawaiian, Tahitian, ethnic, and other foods.

The **Cafe Terrace** at the Mauna Kea Beach Hotel serves the ultimate buffet luncheon on the coast, a feast that visitors to the Big Island should try at least once even though the price is high. The **Pavillion** (882-7222) is on a par, with preparation and presentation of French continental cuisine.

Kailua-Kona: At the **Beach Club** (329-0290) in Kailua-Kona, you can dine on delicious gourmet dishes in a romantic setting amid coconut trees and torches. In a nondescript building, Kuakini Plaza South on Highway 11, **La Bourgogne**'s (329-6711) chef, Guy Chatelard, prepares French dishes comparable to the best on the island.

For the best breakfast in Kailua-Kona, try the **Kona Ranch House** (329-7061, on Kaukini Highway. Where the Oceanview blocks out the view of the ocean and Kailua Pier, **Fisherman's Landing** (326-2555) has to be praised for the most spectacular view of the bay. Sit in one of three outside dining rooms, enjoy the very good food, and most of all the view. The best buffet in South Kona (seafood, $17.95, Fri. Sat., Sun., Chinese, $10.95, Mon.-Thurs.) is at the **Keauhou Beach Hotel** on Alii Drive. The Indonesian **Sibu Cafe** (329-1112) tucked in impersonal Banyan Court offers one of the tastiest and most inexpensive meals in

Kailua-Kona. The **Spinnaker's Sailboat Salad Bar** at
Waterfront Row has the best salad bar in town, sold by
the pound ($3.99). A seaside restaurant with ambience
and romance, outdoor tables and candlelight, is
Jameson's by the Sea (77-6452 Alii Drive, 329-3195),
excellent for steak or seafood. Breakfast or lunch on the
veranda of the **Aloha Theater Cafe** (on Route 11 in
Kainaliu, 322-3383) while gazing onto pastures, coffee
groves, and ocean vistas. The **Oceanview Inn**, Alii
Drive, 329-9998, has a tremendous variety of island and
Chinese dishes for breakfast, lunch, and dinner and specializes in fresh fish. Go early for dinner to avoid
crowds. Delicious Bar-B-Q ribs and chicken, the largest
variety of international beers, and a huge Sunday buffet
in a fun setting at **The Jesters Tavern**, one mile south
of Kailua on Kuakini Highway, 326-7633, is the most
notable recent addition to medium-priced restaurants in
town.

Nightlife
Watching the sunset from the Kailua Pier is a good start.
Check on schedules for local luaus if you haven't seen
them on other islands. At the luau at the **King
Kamehameha** on Sundays, Tuesdays, and Thursdays,
you eat by torchlight at the Kamakahonu restoration.
The luau at the **Kona Village Resort** on Friday nights is
special. The **Kona Surf Hotel** offers a free Polynesian
revue nightly and dancing in the **Puka Bar**. A good
opportunity to visit the **Mauna Kea** and its **Cafe
Terrace** is provided by the luau or nightly Hawaiian
music. The resort's **Batik Room** features dance music.
The jazz band at the bar in the **Mauna Lani Bay Hotel**
provides nightly entertainment. Disco at the chrome
deco **Eclipse Restaurant**, Kuakini Highway across from
Foodland. For live bands in Kailua-Kona, the action is
on Alii Drive at the **Spindrifter**. Even if the soft rock or
jazz music doesn't satisfy you, the views of the bay will.
If there's a moon to watch, take a stroll from the pier
along Alii Drive.

Itinerary Options

If you decide not to take Route 25 to Kohala, there are two more direct routes to Kailua-Kona: 40 miles on **Highway 190** through the tall grass plateau occupied by the Parker Ranch to the flanks of Mount Hualalai on the Hawaii Belt Road, which becomes Palani Road as it heads for Kailua Village; or down Highway 19 to Kawaihae Harbor on the Kona Coast, a faster but much less scenic road than Highway 190. From Highway 190, take Highway 180 (which parallels Highways 19 and 11 but higher up the mountainside) and head for **Holualoa** above Kailua-Kona, a tiny, charming town that has become a remarkable art center.

Scuba and skin diving off the Kona Coast are outstanding from North Kona's Spencer Beach, Hapuna Beach, and 69 Beach to Napoopoo Beach, Pu'uhonua O Honaunau Park, and Hookena Beach in South Kona. The water is very clear and flat, protected from trade winds by Mauna Kea and Mauna Loa. The lava rock reefscapes are home to colorful red pencil urchins, moorish idols, lionfish, butterfly angelfish, green and yellow trumpet-fish, and spotted moray eels. At the **Old Airport Beach**, nudibranchs, cowries, puffers, and scorpionfish hide in the coral heads. If you are a veteran snorkeler or ready to learn, don't miss **Kealakekua Underwater State Park**'s marine preserve, with its myriad tropical fish and spectacular coral growths. Skin diving and scuba diving also are excellent at Hale Halawai, Kahaluu Beach Park, and Napoopoo Beach Park in South Kona. **Honokohau**, two miles north of Kailua, better known for nude sunbathing, has snorkeling, too (stay out of the shark-frequented harbor). Many boat charters leave from Kailua-Kona for diving in the nearby waters. However, for learning about each site's natural and cultural history between two dives, it's hard to find a better experience than **Kona Kai Diving** (P.O. Box 4178, Kailua-Kona, HI 96745, 329-0695).

The 65-foot submarine **Atlantis** (329-6626) takes passengers 80 to 100 feet below Kona Bay to explore an underwater world that even most scuba divers don't see.

The cost of the dive is steep, $67 for adults and $33 for children, and $87 for Wednesday night dives (or day and night dives packaged for $99), but the price is worth the unique experience. (For underwater photography, be sure to bring 400 ASA film.)

About an hour on a **Captain Bean's Cruise** (329-6411), which includes viewing underwater marine life through a glass-bottom boat with hula dancing and entertainment, is $10 for adults, $5 for children. Boats departs daily from Kailua-Kona Pier at 5:15 p.m. for a 2-hour sunset cruise, all-you-can-eat buffet, dance and other music, adults only $42.

The first whales off the Big Island are sighted in November, and whale-watching cruises begin in December. The best whale-watching experience is with research biologist **Dan McSweeney**, who has been researching whales for over 15 years along the Kona Coast. In the past Dan has been on board **Hawaiian Cruises** (329-6411), but he probably has his own boat by now, so track him down.

Marlin fishing and other game fishing off the Kona Coast is reputedly the finest in the world. Charters operating out of Kailua-Kona usually charge $350 for a full eight- to nine-hour day or $85 per person for a half day, four to five hours. Reserve your charter as far ahead as possible, paying a 25 percent deposit. Contact: Kona Coast Activities, 329-3171; Pamela Big Game Fishing, 329-1525; Roy Gay, 329-6041; Kona Charter Skippers' Association, 329-3600; Twin Charter Sportfishing, 329-4753; Seawife Charters, 329-1806; Lucky Lil Sportfishing, 325-5438; Aloha Charter Fishing and Activities, 329-2200; Omega Sport Fishing, 325-7859; or Marlin Country Charters, 326-1666.

With **Captain Zodiac**, you can explore the Kona coastline, from Honokohau Yacht Harbor to Honaunau Bay, in a 23-foot raft, watch humpback whales January to April, and snorkel in Kealakekua Bay, maybe accompanied by spinner dolphins. Two trips a day, 8:00 a.m. to noon and 1:00 to 5:00 p.m., $57 for adults and $47 for children 2-12.

THE BIG ISLAND: KONA COAST

Explore the sun-soaked region of jagged lava fields and tropical waters around the Kona Coast's major resort town, Kailua-Kona. You'll understand why Kamehameha spent the last 7 years of his life beside Kailua Bay. Robert Louis Stevenson saw Kailua Village as "the sleepiest, quietest, Sundayest looking place you can imagine." The town is becoming very commercial very fast and losing charm but still is enjoyable for shopping and historic sights along Alii Drive. Driving down the Kona Coast to the remarkably clear waters of Kealakekua Bay is the best part of the day.

Suggested Schedule

8:30 a.m.	Leisurely breakfast.
9:30 a.m.	Walking tour of Kailua-Kona including the Hotel King Kamehameha, Kailua Pier, Hulihee Palace, and Mokuaikaua Church.
12:00 noon	Picnic lunch at a Kona Beach or lunch at Teshima's Restaurant in Honalo.
1:00 p.m.	Visit the Royal Kona Coffee Mill and Museum.
2:00 p.m.	On the shores of beautiful Kealakekua Bay (or sailing in the bay itself).
3:00 p.m.	Pu'uhonua O Honaunau Park in the City of Refuge National Historical Park.
4:30 p.m.	Visit St. Benedict's Church, Kona's famous "painted church."
6:00 p.m.	Watch the sunset in Kailua before dinner.

Orientation

As you enter Kailua-Kona, Highway 19 becomes Highway 11 a few miles south of the intersection with Palani Road (Highway 190). Palani Road passes two shopping centers before crossing Kuakini Highway to become Alii Drive. Directly ahead on the right, as Alii Drive curves past Kailua Pier, is the Hotel King

Kamehameha. Glass-bottom boat rides, fishing charters, and lunch and dinner cruises sail from the pier into the crystal blue waters of Kailua Bay. Kamakahonu Beach and the lagoon extending from the hotel were the home of King Kamehameha the Great before he died in 1819 and the site of the Ahuena Heiau, now being restored. South of the pier along Alii Drive, the Hulihee Palace and Museum is on the bay side now, and across the street is the 112-foot steeple of Mokuaikaua Church. St. Michael's Church is another 2 miles south, beyond the intersection of Hualalai Road (Route 182) with Alii Drive and Highway 19. Now get in your car and drive south on Alii Drive to Magic Sands Beach for a picnic lunch. And from there take Kam III Road to Highway 11 through the small villages of Honalo, Kainaliu, and Kealakekua, turning to Kealakekua Bay on Napoopoo Road for about 3 miles to Middle Keli Road. Turn right to the Royal Kona Coffee Mill and Museum. From near the mill, follow the winding road down to Kealakekua Bay, where you can see the Captain Cook Monument, a white obelisk at the north base of the cliffs. A rough, unmarked one-lane road continues south through lava fields to Pu'uhonua O Honaunau (City of Refuge) National Historic Park, 29 miles south of Kailua-Kona on Highway 160. Nearby Keei Beach is a secluded gem with wonderful views of Kealakekua Bay. Follow Highway 160 back to Highway 11, and watch for a turnoff to the left for St. Benedict's Church.

Sightseeing Highlights

▲▲▲**King Kamehameha's Royal Palace**—The restored palace grounds adjacent to the Hotel King Kamehameha include Ahuena Heiau, a lava rock platform with thatched buildings and wooden gods on its own small island adjacent to the shore and connected by a footbridge. Free guided tours of the displays and royal grounds are offered Monday through Friday at 1:30 p.m.

▲▲**Hulihee Palace**—A gracious two-story building stands in the middle of town just down Alii Drive from the King Kamehameha Hotel. It was used in the 1880s by

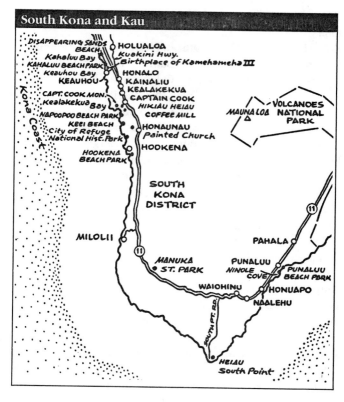

South Kona and Kau

King David Kalakaua as a summer palace. Restored to its former elegance, it features nineteenth-century furnishings and artifacts. The hours are 9:00 a.m. to 4:00 p.m. with a $4 admission fee for adults, $.50 for children.

▲**Mokuaikaua Church**—Directly across Alii Drive from the Hulihee Palace, this is the oldest church in the islands. Completed in 1837, 17 years after the first missionaries arrived, the lava and coral structure with the white steeple is a local landmark.

▲**The Royal Kona Coffee Mill**—On Napoopoo Road near the town of Captain Cook, this mill has been grinding and roasting Kona coffee for nearly a century. The coffee trees are grown on just a few thousand acres, spread over 600 farms between 700 and 2,000 feet, with perfect temperature and soil. A highlight of the visit is the collection of old photographs showing harvests in the days when

"Kona nightingales" (mules) carried the coffee beans to the mill.

▲▲▲Pu'uhonua O Honaunau National Historic Park—Four miles along a rough and bumpy coastal road from Kealakekua Bay is Pu'uhonua O Honaunau National Historical Park. (The other way to reach Pu'uhonua O Honaunau is to drive on Route 11 to mile marker 104 where Route 160 goes down to this historic site.) Just a half-mile down this road, turn right onto a lava bed road for Keei Beach. This narrow salt-and-pepper beach has hardly enough room to pitch a tent, the swimming is decent, but the main attraction is a channel through the coral to an underwater sea grotto. Pu'uhonua O Honaunau Park itself has excellent dive spots.

Entrance to the park is $1 per person, free to those under 16 and over 61. Pick up a brochure from the Visitors Center (328-2288), which is open 7:30 a.m. to 5:30 p.m. daily (but the park doesn't close until midnight).

▲Hikiau Heiau—In Kealakekua Bay is a reconstruction of the temple, Hikiau Heiau, where Captain Cook was killed in 1779. The Captain Cook Monument rises across the bay.

▲St. Benedict's Painted Church—Off Highway 160 (heading up to Highway 11), this church was decorated inside in the early 1900s by Father John Berchmans Velghe, a Belgian priest. The walls, ceiling, and pillars bear copies of medieval religious works and six biblical scenes with Hawaiian motifs, for the benefit of parishioners who couldn't read. From here, Hawaii Volcanoes National Park is about 100 miles, a 3-hour drive that is better left for tomorrow.

Where to Stay

Past Kona Kai Farms, on your left, between the old white gas station and Sakamoto Electric (between the 110 and 111 mile markers), turn uphill 0.2 mile and then make a left on a paved road for about 350 feet to **Merryman's B&B**, P.O. Box 474, Kealakekua, HI 86750 (323-2276, $65-$80 double).

This is a new house in a lush setting. You'll find comfort, privacy, an excellent breakfast, and a central location for visiting attractions from Kailua-Kona to Captain Cook.

A step up from the Kona Hotel and Teshima's but still in the budget category, the **Manago Hotel** (P.O. Box 145, Captain Cook, HI 96704, 323-2642) on Highway 11 in Captain Cook has 42 individual accommodations, some with a great ocean view and their own bathrooms in the newer wing for $29 to $32 single and $35 to $55 double.

On Highway 11, the fifth house on the right after the green 103 mile marker is **Adrienne and Reg Ritz-Batty's B&B** (85-4577 Mamalahoa Hwy., R.R. 1, Box 8E, Captain Cook, HI 96704, 800-242-0039 or 328-9726, $50 to $70 single or double, and a loft for $35 with a shared bath). From their lanai in back of the house, you have an unobstructed view of the slopes above the City of Refuge and the ocean. This B&B is an excellent base for exploring the South Kona area or an overnight stay before heading for South Point and Volcano.

Where to Eat

South of Holualoa, past the Hualalai Road junction, after winding through coffee groves on both sides of the road you arrive at Kuakini Highway (11). Both Mamalahoa Highway and Kuakini Highway take you to **Honalo**. The town's claim to fame is unpretentious, booth-lined **Teshima's** (Highway 11, Honalo, HI 96750, 332-9140), which has been open continuously since 1943. Breakfast is served starting at 6:30 a.m.

In **Kainaliu**, about a half mile from Teshima's, very visible on the makai side of Highway 19 as you enter town, is the **Aloha Theater Cafe**. Between 8:00 a.m. and 8:00 p.m. (except Sunday, when Kainaliu is shut down), the Aloha Cafe serves real Kona coffee (versus diluted blends), huge healthy salads, tasty vegetarian meals, great corn bread and whole grain pancakes, smoothies, carrot cake, and other pastries, at reasonable prices.

Itinerary Options

Sightseeing in Kainalu and Kealakekua: Just past the former Fujino Mill (one of Kona's oldest, operated by the Captain Cook Coffee Company), visit **Tom Kadaooka's** for orchids. Less than a mile south of Kealakekua on

Highway 11, the historic **Greenwell Store** of the former Greenwell Ranch coffee operation houses the **Kona Historical Society Museum**. Built in the mid-1800s by H. N. Greenwell, the masonry uses native stone joined with lime made from burned coral. The museum's reference library and archive contains photographs, manuscripts, maps, and a few artifacts of old Kona that can be examined 9:00 a.m. to 3:00 p.m. on weekdays.

At the **Captain Cook Coffee Company** building, near Honaunau, enjoy a free fresh-brewed cup of Kona coffee along with a breathtaking view of Kealakekua Bay. Afterward drive south on Highway 11 and stop at **Mrs. Fields Macadamia Nut Factory**, the **Honwanji Buddhist Temple**, the **Central Kona Union Church**, or the **Lanakila** and **Christ churches**. Head down Napoopoo Road to **Kealakekua Bay**. This zigzagging road passes the **Royal Kona Coffee Mill and Museum**. The nearby **Mauna Kea Mill and Museum** (328-2511) also tells the story of Kona coffee processing to frequent waves of tour buses and vans. If you're not ready for more coffee, wait for **Kona Kai Farms**, just before the turnoff to Kealakekua Bay, or **Bong Brothers Coffee Company**, a mile before Pu'uhonua Road (Route 160).

At the bottom of the hill is **Napoopoo**, a former fishing village, and Kealakekua (Road of the God) Bay at road's end. The bay is a Marine Life Conservation District with a fine beach and fantastic snorkeling out of **Napoopoo Beach Park**. In a picturesque setting with cliffs surrounding the harbor, Napoopoo Beach Park has good swimming and excellent diving. Diving is even better near the **Captain Cook Monument** at the northern end of the bay. (Don't swim over in the early evening when sharks come to feed.) Near the park's parking lot is the well-preserved **Hikiau Heiau**, dedicated to the god Lono, carved into the pali with a marvelous view of the bay.

Instead of returning to Kailua-Kona, continue south on Highway 11 to mile marker 77. Shortly thereafter, turn left on Donala Street to Bruce and Robin Hall's **South Point Bed & Breakfast** (Hei 92-1408 Donala Drive, Captain Cook, 96704, 929-7466), midway between Kona and

Volcano. Singles and doubles are $60 per night. Volcano is an easy 45-minute drive away. The best-kept secret in this area is the **Road to the Sea**, two beaches (Humuhumu Point and Awili Point) at the end of a seven-mile-long cinder road. The road leads to several cinder cones and these green-tinted black sand beaches. Drive slowly and then park above the last slope. Trails offer hiking possibilities for panoramic views.

Vast tracts of lava rubble in South Kona give way to high forests on the slopes of Mauna Loa becoming green pasturelands edged by black sand beaches in the Kau District. The narrow road to South Point branches off Highway 11 six miles west of **Naalehu**. Experts dispute when the first ancient Polynesians arrived here—A.D. 700, 300, or even 150. Once the most populated part of the island chain, few people live here now.

South Point Road passes through about 12 miles of grassland, roaming cattle and horses, and the **Kamoa Wind Farm**, to the southernmost point in Hawaii and the nation.

From the **Kaulana Boat Ramp** at South Point, it's 2½ rough miles along the waterline to reach **Green Sand Beach** over a rutted road requiring four-wheel drive or two feet supplied with good hiking boots. Hiking round-trip takes two hours. This volcanic sand beach acquires a greenish tint from olivines eroding from the cinder hill, **Puu Mahana**, behind the beach. Avoid climbing down the cinder cone since it crumbles easily underfoot.

The countryside and its small country towns convey the feeling of an earlier, quieter, more peaceful era. Returning to the Belt Road, pass through **Waiohinu**, past a monkey-pod tree growing from the roots of one planted by Mark Twain in 1866 which was downed by high winds in 1957.

Six miles past the turnoff to South Point is **Naalehu**, with the distinction of the nation's southernmost town. A former plantation town with a touch of cosmopolitan feeling, Naalehu is situated against a backdrop of very scenic hills.

THE BIG ISLAND: SOUTH KONA TO HAWAII VOLCANOES NATIONAL PARK

Drive south from Kailua-Kona along Highway 11 through a landscape that changes every few miles. Rounding the southern tip of the United States, South Point, the volcanic shoreline exposes the work of the fire goddess, Pele, who chose Mauna Loa and Kilauea to show the world her powers. Today these two volcanoes comprise Hawaii Volcanoes National Park. Plan ahead and make reservations at the Kilauea Lodge for a two-night stay adjacent to the park.

Suggested Schedule

7:00 a.m.	Breakfast, check out of Kailua and an early drive to Hawaii Volcanoes National Park.
8:30 a.m.	Visit Milolii.
9:30 a.m.	Manuka State Park.
10:00 a.m.	Optional South Point side trip.
10:45 a.m.	Punaluu Beach.
12:00 noon	Check in at the Kilauea Lodge.
12:30 p.m.	Lunch.
1:30 p.m.	Kilauea Visitor's Center.
2:30 p.m.	Crater Rim Road tour to Thurston Lava Tube, Devastation Trail, and Halemaumau Trail.
6:30 p.m.	Dine at the Kilauea Lodge.

Driving Route

The 53-mile drive from Kailua-Kona to South Point (Ka Lae) past Honaunau passes through land covered with vegetation except for patches or swaths of lava flow. Past Hookena, Highway 11 crosses the 1919, 1936, and 1950 Mauna Loa lava flows and passes a huge macadamia nut orchard. A narrow, winding, bumpy, six-mile spur road leads down to Milolii, a Hawaiian-Filipino fishing community about 2,000 feet below the highway.

The next stopping place, 41 miles from Kailua, is the Manuka State Park. From there, the Belt Road follows the old Mamalahoa Trail 12 miles to the turnoff to South Point Road. It's another 12 miles through flat treeless terrain, down a narrow paved road. Through Waiohinu, Naalehu, and Ninole, it's only a short side trip to Punaluu Beach Park's black sand beach. Beyond Pahala's Ka'u Sugar Mill and its tall smokestack, the countryside turns to rolling green hills and sugarcane fields, macadamia nut orchards, and beautiful valleys with ohia forests. After you pass the Volcano Golf Course, you'll approach Hawaii Volcanoes National Park. Proceed to the marked turnoff from Highway 11 to the Kilauea Visitor's Center.

Sightseeing Highlights

▲▲**Milolii**—Five miles off Route 11 south of Kailua, this is an authentic South Seas fishing village with marvelous tide pools. Built on lava rubble, this active fishing village's houses of old lumber and corrugated iron are relics of a past era. Outrigger canoes are powered by outboards, but the method of fishing for opelu, a type of mackerel, hasn't changed.

▲**Manuka State Park**—On Route 11 south of Milolii is a lovely botanic park several thousand feet above the ocean.

▲▲**Punaluu Beach Park**—One mile off Route 11 north of Naalehu (the "southernmost town in the U.S.A.") is a beautiful black sand beach in a palm-fringed lagoon setting, with a visitor's center, a museum, and nearby Sea Mountain resort with the Punaluu Black Sands Restaurant overlooking the beach. Camping is allowed with a permit. To escape tourist crowds, head about one-third mile south to Ninole Cove for more privacy. On the hill above the beach is a tiny church with a shrine in its graveyard to Henry Opukahaia, the Punaluu boy who sailed to America in 1809 and persuaded Christian missionaries to come to save the souls of his people.

▲▲▲**Hawaii Volcanoes National Park**—Two active volcanoes are here: Mauna Loa, 13,677 feet high and the most massive mountain on earth, and Kilauea Caldera, 4,000 feet, tucked into Mauna Loa's side and encircled by the 11-

mile Crater Rim Drive. The volcano is legendary Pele's home, which for many residents of Hawaii (and not just Hawaiians) is not merely mythology. After Pele was flooded out of Kauai by her sister, the sea goddess, Namalaokahai, for seducing her husband, and was ravished by the Pig God, Kamapua, she made her home in Halemaumau Crater in the Kilauea Caldera. For at least a thousand years, Hawaiians appeased Pele with sacrificial offerings of pigs, dogs, humans, and sacred ohelo berries. In the early 1820s, after the kapus were abandoned, chieftess Kapiolani climbed down into the crater, defied Pele, and claimed the crater for Jehovah, her newly adopted Christian God.

The world's most active volcano, Kilauea last spewed fountains of lava thousands of feet in 1959-60 and pushed lava through underground tunnels to consume the village of Kapoho, 30 miles away. Kilauea fountained again in 1983-84, and Mauna Loa also erupted once more in 1984 after nine quiescent years, the first simultaneous eruption of Kilauea and Mauna Loa in 65 years.

In 1986, lava destroyed homes in Kapaahu and Kalapana Gardens, crossed Highway 130 several times, destroyed ancient Punaluu Heiau, historic Queen's Bath, and poured into the sea. Lava flow from Kilauea in 1990 destroyed most of the remaining homes in Kapaahu and many homes in Kalapana Gardens. Lava continues to flow incessantly from Kilauea.

Kilauea's accessibility has earned it the nickname of the "drive-in volcano." It erupts about every 10 months. (If it erupts while you're in the vicinity, watch out for the tour buses rather than the lava flow.) The 344-square-mile park has two entrances on the flanks of Mauna Loa: the east entrance, from Highway 11, 30 miles directly southwest of Hilo; and the southwest entrance on Highway 11. Both arrive at the Kilauea Visitor's Center (967-7311).

Approaching the park on Route 11 from South Point, about a mile after crossing the park boundary you reach a trailhead and also a very worthwhile side trip: the two-mile Kau Desert Trail (no longer Footprints Trail).

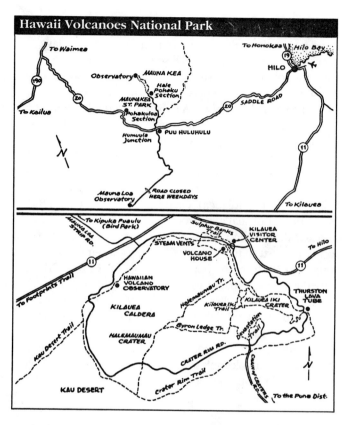

Hawaii Volcanoes National Park

Continuing on Route 11 past the turnoff to Namakani Paio Campground is the Mauna Loa Strip Road to the Tree Molds. Lava flowing through an ohia forest encircled and ignited tree trunks, leaving holes in the ground, some of them quite deep. Tree Molds resembles a reverse of Lava Tree State Park to the east in Punain; in other words, pits instead of tree stumps.

A little farther along the same road is Kipuka Puaulu or Bird Park, a forested area and bird sanctuary with more than 20 species of trees and a one-mile-long self-guided nature trail running through it. One of the loveliest spots on the Big Island, this sanctuary for birds and plant life a few miles up Mauna Loa Road contains one of the finest and most varied examples of native Hawaiian forest.

▲▲▲**Crater Rim Drive**—Circling the Kilauea Crater, this drive passes through 11 miles of rain forest, desert, lava flows, and pumice piles. You'll see two types of lava: smooth-looking ropy lava called *pahoehoe* and, lower down the slope, the rough cindery type known as *aa.*

▲▲**Thurston Lava Tube**—A short trail through the most accessible lava tunnel (450 feet long and 10 feet high), this lava tube is enclosed at the entrance and exit by a fern jungle.

▲▲**Devastation Trail**—This half-mile elevated boardwalk crosses a desolate black lava field through a skeletal forest of ohia tree trunks entombed during the 1959 eruption of Kilauea Iki (Little Kilauea). Gradually returning to life, the trees sprout unusual aerial roots.

▲▲▲**Halemaumau Trail**—This trail can be entered from 2 locations: next to the Visitor's Center, for a 6-mile, 5-hour round trip; or from the opposite side of Crater Rim Drive, where it's only a quarter mile down. Today the shorter walk fits in better. Before leaving this area, visit the Thomas A. Jagger Museum (967-7643), in a former volcano observatory on the crater rim, which opens up a great view of Halemaumau Crater. In the museum, a series of exhibits on the history and volcanology of Mauna Loa and Kilauea provides a much better understanding of what you're about to see (or have just seen).

Where to Stay

Three B&Bs secluded in Volcano Village provide the best variety of B&B choices in one place in all Hawaii. **My Island B&B** (P.O. Box 100, Volcano, HI 96785, 967-7216) is a historic 100-year-old home sitting in a marvelous tropical garden. Rates range from $30 shared bath to $55 private studio with bath. **Volcano B&B** (P.O. Box 22, Volcano, HI 96785, Konelehua and Wright roads in Volcano, 967-7779) has 3 rooms with shared bath, 2 up and 1 down, that range from $45 to $55 depending on season and number in the party. **Chalet Kilauea B&B**'s (P.O. Box 998, Volcano Village, HI 96785, 967-7786, 800-937-7786, $75 double) 3 guest rooms come with a hot tub on the deck and the kind of decor and pampering you'd expect at twice the price. **Kilauea Lodge** (and restaurant, see below; P.O. Box 116, Volcano Village,

96785, 967-7366), located one mile (Hilo-side) from Hawaii Volcanoes National Park, offers uniquely decorated rooms with fireplaces, private baths, and one of the best B&B breakfasts on the Big Island, from $85 to $125. It was built in 1938 as a YMCA camping and lodging facility, and recently Albert and Lorna Jeyte remodeled the lodge and restaurant. Seven new rooms will be added (in a new complex) to the 4 existing rooms of one of the best B&Bs in Hawaii. **Carson's Volcano Cottages** have some of the coziest cottages in one of the loveliest landscaped settings on the Big Island. After a day at the volcano and some time in their hot tub under the stars, you feel at peace with the world. Rates are only $55 to $75 for two. Contact Tom Carson, P.O. Box 503, Volcano, HI 96785, 967-7683.

Namakini Palo Campground (Hawaii Volcanoes National Park, HI 96718, 967-7321) behind the Hawaii Volcano Observatory requires a permit from Park Head-quarters to camp free for up to 7 days. Cabins can be rented through Volcano House for $24 to $31 for up to four people, including sheets, pillows, towel, soap, and blanket. **Kipuka Nene**, 10 miles south of Park Headquarters, also requires a permit and is free. The **Niaulani Cabin**, rented by the Division of State Parks, Hilo, on Old Volcano Road about a half mile from the Volcano General Store, costs from $10 for a single person to $60 for six people.

Where to Eat
Right at the beach, the **Punaluu Black Sands Restaurant**, 928-8528, has lunches and dinners at moderate to expensive prices. Pick up a take-out snack lunch to eat in the picnic area at Bird Park Trail. The nearby **Sea Mountain Golf Course & Lounge**, Punaluu, 928-6222, serves a simple breakfast and lunch and dinner with excellent views of the volcanoes over the golf course. About 2 miles from the park in Volcano Village, you have three choices. At the gourmet **Lodge Restaurant**, 967-7366, try the seafood Mauna Kea or the Fettuccini Primavera, with Kilauea Lodge coffee for dessert and Sunday Surprise at the marvelous Sunday brunch, 10:30 a.m. to 2:30 p.m., closed for lunch in off-season. Reservations essential

HAWAII VOLCANOES NATIONAL PARK

The 54-mile round-trip drive on the Chain of Craters Road to the coast, which passes fingers of lava, lava fields, and pit craters, traces the history of lava flows for centuries. After seeing a film describing the origins and history of Hawaii's volcanoes, follow the Road as far as Park Rangers say is permissible. Return to the Visitors Center and take Route 11 two miles west to the Mauna Loa Strip Road. Drive up to a unique nature sanctuary (*kipuka*), which also is an ideal picnic spot. After lunch, walk around the lovely 1.1-mile loop nature trail, and then continue up the Strip Road to a lookout at 6,700 feet up Mauna Loa for panoramic views of the park. Return to Highway 11 and the Volcano Art Center to see one of Hawaii's best collections of local arts and crafts.

Suggested Schedule

9:00 a.m.	See film about park geology and volcanic activity at the Visitor's Center and take a self-guided tour in the museum.
10:00 a.m.	Drive Chain of Craters Road.
12:30 p.m.	Mauna Loa Road to Bird Park.
1:00 p.m.	Picnic lunch in Bird Park.
2:00 p.m.	Walk on Bird Park trail.
2:30 p.m.	Continue up Mauna Loa Road to Overlook.
4:00 p.m.	Browse at the Volcano Art Center.
5:00 p.m.	Return to Volcano House or elsewhere for some refreshments for cleanup and a change of clothing.
6:30 p.m.	Dinner and an evening of relaxation.

Sightseeing Highlights

▲▲▲**The Kilauea Visitor Center** (open 7:45 a.m. to 5:00 p.m., 967-7311) is an essential stop for maps and books, and a film shown daily on the hour, starting at 9:00 a.m., explains how volcanoes are formed and traces the eruptions that began in 1986. The park entrance fee is $5 per car.

▲▲**Chain of Craters Road** winds 27 miles down the southern slopes of Kilauea Volcano to the ruins of the Wahaula Visitor Center on the Puna Coast. There is no water or gas along this paved two-lane road. You'll see wonderful vistas of the coastline, fingers of aa and pahoehoe lava reaching down to the sea, and craters with different stages of life, from none to thickly forested ones.

▲▲**Mauna Loa Road**—Follow Highway 11 past the Sulphur Banks and the Volcano Golf Course (away from the volcano center) to the Mauna Loa Strip Road. This road takes you up to Kipuka Puaulu (Bird Park), an oasis created when the Mauna Loa lava flow divided and left about 100 acres of native plants untouched. The park contains picnic grounds, exhibits about the park's plants and birds, a mile-long nature trail among some of the world's rarest plants, and a bird sanctuary. Continue along the 10-mile paved road up to the 6,682-foot level to a parking area and lookout. The road then climbs 18.3 miles to the south rim of Moku'aweoweo Caldera at 13,250 feet.

▲**Volcano Art Center**—This art center, housed in the original Volcano House, sells local paintings, handicrafts, and jewelry from 8:30 a.m. to 5:00 p.m. The selection is the best on the island for Big Island art.

▲**Sulphur Banks**—Here, Kilauea releases water into cracks or fumaroles to rise as sulfur gases. The nearby Steam Vents don't contain the sulfur.

▲▲**Halemaumau Crater**—Just past the Hawaiian Volcano Observatory, this crater steams and shows its latent power. Along the trail a series of plaques tells about the area's geology and history.

▲▲**The Kau Desert Footprints Trail**—This trail is on Route 11 about 4 miles south of the Mauna Loa Road. The 1.6-mile round-trip leads across desolate pahoehoe and aa to where about 80 warriors were crossing the desert to battle Kamehameha's warriors when Kilauea erupted. Toxic gases engulfed them and killed them in their tracks. This incredible event was seen as a sign from the gods, endorsing Kamehameha.

THE BIG ISLAND: RETURN TO HILO FOR DEPARTURE TO KAUAI

Drive to Keaau and then to the Puna Coast through Pahoa, the anthurium and papaya capital of Hawaii. From Pahoa, Route 132 leads along a beautiful stretch of tree-lined road to the Lava Tree State Monument. Plan to stop frequently along Puna's scenic coastline, and include a picnic lunch. En route to Hilo, visit the world's largest macadamia nut processor. Return to Hilo's General Lyman Airport, turn in your rental car, and take an early evening flight to Kauai's Lihue Airport.

Suggested Schedule

8:00 a.m.	Breakfast
9:00 a.m.	Departure for Puna District.
10:00 a.m.	Sightseeing in Pahoa.
10:30 a.m.	Drive to Lava Tree State Park.
11:30 a.m.	Coastal sightseeing and visit to Cape Kumukahi Lighthouse.
12:30 noon	Picnic lunch along the Puna Coast.
2:30 p.m	Visit the Mauna Loa Macadamia Nut Orchards and Mill in Keaau.
3:30 p.m.	Return to Hilo for departure to Kauai. Drop off car at the airport or in town.
5:00 p.m.	Flight to Lihue Airport, Kauai.
6:25 p.m.	Arrive in Lihue and pick up your rental car at the airport.
7:15 p.m.	Check into your Lihue or Wailua-Kapaa accommodations.
7:45 p.m.	Enjoy dinner and evening entertainment.

Orientation—Puna

Since 1987, it hasn't been possible to drive from the Chain of Craters Road to the Puna Coast. The park's south entrance, the Waha'ula Visitors Center at the intersection of Route 130, and Chain of Craters Road have been blocked by successive lava flows. Get the latest reports of lava flows from National Park Rangers before heading to the Puna end of Route 137. From Volcano, it's 19 miles to **Keaau**. At mile marker 22½ on Highway 11 on the right side of the road, a few miles beyond Glenwood, is **Akatsuka Tropical Orchids and Flower Gardens** (967-7660), open 8:30 a.m. to 5:00 p.m. A dozen mixed sizes of anthuriums shipped Federal Express to the mainland costs only about $25.

Turn right on Rt. 130 to **Pahoa**. The former ranchland between Keeau and Pahoa was sold off as vacation lots in 1950, and parts of it have become suburbs of Hilo known as Hawaiian Paradise Park and Orchid Land Estates. Black netting over anthurium nurseries seen as you approach Pahoa, a former lumber and then sugar town, announce the anthurium (and papaya) capital of Hawaii and the world.

At the junction of Routes 130 and 11, this is the home of the **Mauna Loa Macadamia Nut Orchards and Mill**, the world's largest producer and processor of macadamia nuts. Enjoy free samples, watch mill operations, or buy gift boxes before heading for Hilo.

Sightseeing Highlights
▲**Pahoa**—Pahoa is quaint and ramshackle, colorful and drab. Stop even for a few minutes to walk along the raised wooden sidewalks in front of false-front shops. At shops selling local fruit and vegetables, pick up a picnic lunch. Pahoa is the kind of town where you can even order tofu enchiladas—at Paradise West—for breakfast (unless for some reason you prefer whole grain pancakes and eggs). In the past, Pahoa has been bypassed by heavy bus traffic heading on Route 130 to Kaimu Black Sand Beach. Now, with Kaimu filled with lava, even that magnet for traffic is gone. The Pahao Artist's and Crafts Guild (965-7335), a cooperative venture of about 20 artists, is the only outlet outside of Hilo and Volcano on this side of the island that displays the work of local artists.

The first anthurium plants arrived in Hawaii from London over 100 years ago. With proper care, anthuriums will last 3 to 4 weeks as cut flowers. Visit the Hawaiian

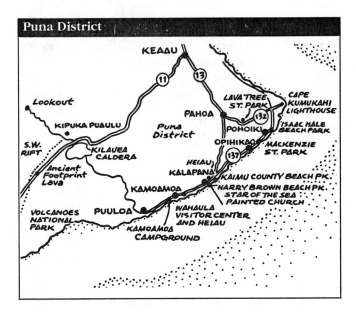

Greenhouse (965-8351) or Hawaiian Anthuriums of
Pahoa (965-8247). More than 100 genera and 2,000
species of anthuriums in the Araceae family (a "cousin"
of philodendrons) can be seen at these two greenhouses.
▲▲**Lava Tree State Monument**—The pahoehoe lava
that poured through this ohia forest in 1790 left hardened
tree-shaped shells after cooling which today stand in the
midst of lovely new lehua tree growth. A loop of less
than a mile circles through the park, passing numerous
wild tropical plants and flowers when they're in bloom.
(Bring mosquito repellent with you.)
▲▲**Cape Kumukahi Lighthouse**—Route 132 ends 10
miles from Pahoa at Cape Kumukahi (First Beginning).
Along the way, *HVB Warriors* mark the lava flows of
1955 and 1960. The 1960 Puna eruption, on the east rift
of Kilauea, 28 miles from the Kilauea Caldera, destroyed
70 buildings in Kapoho and added 500 acres to Puna.
The former sugar town of Kapoho that used to border
both sides of Route 137 no longer exists; it is covered by
lava that erupted for 31 days from the cinder cone. Stay
on Route 132 (Kapoho Road) across Route 137 to Cape
Kumukahi, turn left to the Kukii Heiau site, adjacent to a

memorial for a burial ground itself buried by the 1960 lava flow. Continue to the end of this cinder road to Cape Kumukahi Lighthouse, amazingly spared by Madame Pele's lava flow, which split around the lighthouse. Local legend says that on the fateful night in 1960 when lava spared the lighthouse, Pele, disguised as an old woman begging for food, was befriended by the lighthousekeeper and turned away by residents of devastated Kapoho.

▲▲▲**Puna Coast**—Take a right on Pohoiki Road just past Lava Tree and you'll pass the controversial geothermal power station, which may or may not be in operation depending on politics and economic feasibility. Pohoiki Road brings you to the coast at Isaac Hale Beach Park. The main attraction of Isaac Hale is a volcanically heated freshwater pond. Camping (with precautions) is preferable in the ironwood grove at beautiful MacKenzie State Park. bordered by black lava seacliffs. Visit these parks after taking a short but worthwhile side trip. At the intersection of Routes 132 and 137, take a right if you are coming from the lighthouse (or a left if traveling from Pahoa) on paved Old Government Road, which shortly turns to a single-lane packed dirt road. Drive 1.5 miles on this road through beautiful hau jungle to a turnoff to your right between two large mango trees. Return to Route 137 and drive down the coast to the Kapoho Tidepools for excellent snorkeling.

▲▲**Kehena Beach**—Three miles from the more famous Kaimu Black Sand Beach, wiped out by volcanic flow in 1990-91, Kehena's beach actually consists of two black sand pockets. There's good shore fishing for ulua, papio, mountain bass, red bigeye, and other fish, but the beach is dangerous for swimming and snorkeling. For picnicking, head for a smaller back sand beach on the northern end of the Kehena, more protected and partially shaded by coconut trees (and especially favored by nude bathers). After lunch, backtrack to Opihikao Road and turn left to return to Route 130, Pahao and Keaau to Highway 11 and either Hilo or Volcano. Nearby Kahuwai, one of the best-kept secrets on the Puna Coast, is a former center for canoe building and residence of alii. The beautiful black sand beach formed by the 1960 Kapoho lava flow is tucked between two low seacliffs on the rugged shoreline pounded year-round by surf. The area has many sites of historical and archaeological interest.

Iniki Update

Severely damaged by Hurricane Iniki in September 1992, as of early 1993, some resorts, hotels, B&Bs, and other facilities for visitors are back in business. The Kauai chapter of the Hawaii Visitors Bureau is publishing the *Hurricane Iniki Recovery Update* (call 800-262-1400 or fax 800-637-5762), and you can get information about every hotel and service on the island. By the end of 1993, all visitors' facilities on Kauai should be back in full operation.

Getting to Kauai

The Richard A. Kawakami Terminal opened in 1987. This airport continues to be expanded and upgraded into the mid-1990s. Hawaiian Airlines has a one-stop (Honolulu) flight leaving Hilo for Lihue Airport, Kauai, at 5:00 p.m., arriving on Kauai at 6:25 p.m. Aloha Airlines has flights at 5:15 p.m., 6:15 p.m., and 6:40 p.m. With one and two stops and change of planes, these flights take close to 2 hours.

Getting around Kauai

From the terminal, you can get bus or limousine service to all hotels for between $7 and $25. Check with Gray Line Kauai (245-3344), Kauai Island Tours (245-4777), Robert's Hawaii Tours (245-9558) or Trans-Hawaiian Kauai (245-5108). The cost of a taxi (Aloha Taxi, 245-4609) to your hotel versus a bus or limousine also surprisingly is negligible. Poipu Beach costs about $30; Coco Palms resort, about $20.

Otherwise, most people will rent a car from a major U-drive company or a local company. The difference in cost between national and local companies is negligible, especially if you make reservations beforehand. You'll need a rental car for active sightseeing on Kauai.

Across the street from the terminal at Lihue Airport is a string of car rental booths. Car rentals with a flat rate start at $21.95 a day, unlimited mileage. Rent-A-Wreck, Rent-A-Jeep Kauai, 245-9622, and Beach Boy, 245-2913 in Lihue and Westside, 332-8644 in Kalaheo, have rentals at $16.95 or lower but may tack on a mileage charge. You won't need a four-wheel drive on Kauai.

Biking around Kauai is easy except for Kokee, the narrow shoulders on the roads, and increasingly heavy traffic. Cycling on Highways 50 and 56 (the Belt Road) is downright hazardous. Rental shops are Bicycles Kauai, 1379 Kuhio Highway, in Kapaa, 822-3315, Aquatics Kauai, Kapaa, 822-9213; Peddle & Paddle, Hanalei, 826-9069; and South Shore Activities, next to the Sheraton in Poipu, 742-6873. Rentals cost $4 per hour or $12 to $20 per day or $100 per week.

Where to Stay

The least expensive, simplest, down-to-earth hotels, motels, and apartments, mostly family run, are in Lihue, Kauai's biggest town and the seat of government. Budget accommodations are even more plentiful here than in Hilo, with lots of small, basic, quiet, clean rooms with ceiling fans but no telephones or TVs. Rates are as low as $20 to $30 for single and double rooms. The best budget deals in Lihue with kitchenettes or kitchens are at **Hale Lihue Hotel**, 2931 Kalena Street off Rice, 245-3151, a pink, 2-story, very basic budget "motel" with 22 one-bedrooms for $55. Other budget choices are **Hale Pumehana Motel**, at 3083 Akahi Street, which has 17 units at $27 to $35 for a 1-bedroom and a refrigerator, across from the Lihue Shopping Center, Box 1828, 245-2106; and **Ocean View Motel**, on the corner of Rice Street and Wilcox Road, 3445 Wilcox Road, Nawiliwili, 245-6345, pink again, seedy-looking outside but spotless inside, $35 for two.

The best moderate-priced choices in Wailua close to the beach are the **Kauai Sands Hotel**, 420 Papaloa Road, Kapaa, 800-367-7000 or 822-4951, next to the Coconut Plantation Marketplace (Lihue side), 201 recently renovated rooms, $60 for single or double standard rooms or a special package of $79 to $97 for two with a budget car and unlimited mileage; and, right on the beach near the Coconut Plantation, the **Kapaa Sands**, 380 Papaloa Road, Kapaa, 882-4901 or 800-222-4901, a condo with $75 to $85 studios with kitchens, 3-night minimum in summer, 7 days in winter. The **Kauai Beach Boy**, 484 Kuhio Hwy., #100, Kapaa, 822-3441 or 800-922-7866, on Waipouli Beach, offers a studio at $80. The off-season price for an ocean-front studio apartment at the **Mokihana of Kauai**, 796 Kuhio Highway, 822-3971, is $60 per night for a single or double room. The oceanfront 2-bedroom duplexes are $80. Farther up Highway 96 in Kapaa, the **Hotel Coral Reef**, 1516 Kuhio Highway, 822-4481 or 800-843-4569, is also on the ocean with its own beach, close to a good swimming beach and restaurants. Comfortable but spare 1-bedrooms in the old wing are $41 to $67, and upper rooms in the new wing with ocean views start at $75 single or double.

The **Coco Palms Resort Hotel**, 800-542-2626 or 822-4921, was one of the first hotels built on the island. With 35 acres of coconut trees and a nightly torch lighting ceremony, it's a popular tourist destination. The coconut grove gardens and lagoon together with the Polynesian and longhouse decor of the lobby and restaurants give the Coco Palms a distinctive and memorable atmosphere. Rates start at $110 per night.

Where to Eat

Some of the best budget eating places in Lihue are in and around the Lihue Shopping Center. Big breakfasts for under $2 or Hawaiian dinners, like kalua pork with two eggs and lomi salmon, for under $3, at **Ma's Family**, 4277 Halenani Street at the corner of Kress, 245-3142, will spoil you for the rest of the trip. Saimin, with noodles, slivers of meat and fish, vegetables, wonton, and eggs in a delicious broth, costs less than $3 at **Hamamura Saimin Stand**, 2956 Kress Street, 245-3271, around the corner from Ma's.

Two restaurants in the Haleko Shops, across from the Lihue Shopping Center, will take care of those looking for big breakfasts, meat dinners, and Italian food: omelets at **Eggberts**, 245-6325; and manicotti or cannelloni at **Casa Italiana**, 245-9586. After serving steak in garlic and wine sauce for 20 years in Lihue, **J. J. Broiler**, 246-4422, moved to the Anchor Cove Shopping Center. The restaurant now occupies two floors overlooking Kalapahi Beach next to the mammoth new Westin Kauai.

In Kapaa, **Al & Dons**, 822-4221, in the Kauai Sands Hotel, south of the Plantation Marketplace in Coconut Plantation, is one of the better restaurant deals, especially for breakfast. For a fresh fish dinner (or buffalo meat) at a moderate price, try the **Ono Family Restaurant**, 4-1292 Kuhio Highway, 822-1710, in the center of Kapaa, or the **Kapaa Fish & Chowder House**, 1639 Kuhio Highway, 822-7488, not far from the Hotel Coral Reef. The **Kountry Kitchen**, 1485 Kuhio Highway, 822-3511, serves hefty breakfasts. For Hawaiian food (laulau, lomi salmon, kalua pig) at reasonable prices, visit the **Aloha Diner** in the Waipouli complex, 4-971 Kuhio Highway, 822-3851.

Nightlife

The place to go in Lihue for disco and live music Wednesday through Saturday after 10:00 p.m. is the **Club Jetty Restaurant**, 245-4970, in Nawiliwili. Or, your excuse for visiting the Westin Kauai Hotel in Nawiliwili could be dancing at **The Paddling Club**, a 3-level disco. In Kapaa and Wailua, if you have the energy, you can dance until 4:00 a.m. at the **Vanishing Point**'s disco in Waipouli Plaza or to live music at the **Kauai Beach Boy's Boogie Palace**. Time for another or one last luau? Try the **Sheraton Coconut Beach**, 822-3455, or the **Aston Kauai Resort Hotel**, 245-3931, for live entertainment a few nights a week.

Itinerary Options

You may decide to stay overnight or longer in Puna, especially when you see the accommodation choices. Just two blocks from the lighthouse turnoff on the left (toward Kalapana) is the entrance to Kapoho Beach Road and two private homes at **Champagne Cove**. This is one of the loveliest, most unspoiled getaway vacation spots on the Big Island. If you like privacy, comfort, feeding friendly sea turtles, picking bananas off trees in your yard, and a warm tide pool and swimming pool at the doorstep to your three-bedroom oceanfront house, then call **Dr. Keith or Norma Godfrey** (1714 Lei Lelua St., Hilo, 96720, 959-4487, $75 per day, three-day minimum). About five miles north of Kalapana is a unique retreat, cultural center, and health spa for "New Age" vegetarian travelers: **Kalani Honua** (Box 4500, Pahoa, HI 96778, 965-7828). Children are very welcome at this 20-acre oceanfront center. Activities and services include yoga classes, a summer camp, a dance program, resident artists, language courses, and business training. The communal atmosphere is very relaxed. Facilities include a swimming pool, Japanese spa area with sauna, classrooms, massage available, bicycle tours, and four cedar lodges with cooking facilities, private or shared baths, private rooms, and a relatively new three-bedroom, two-bath guest house that sleeps six. A room with a shared bath for three nights or more is $52 a night single or double, $62 to $75 with private bath, $85 for a cottage.

Kauai Canoe Expeditions, 245-5122, at the Kauai Canoe Club, near the Menehune Fishpond, and **Island Adventures**, both in Nawiliwili, 245-9662, will take you canoeing for 2 hours up the Huleia River and along the fish pond into a wildfowl refuge. **Kauai by Kayak**, 245-9662, offers the same trip. **Kauai River Expeditions**, 826-9608, instructs you in the use of a combined canoe and kayak called a royak, then leads you up the Kalihi Wai River. For other outfitters that run guided one-day or longer sea-kayak trips along Kauai's Na Pali coastline include **Outfitters Kauai** in Poipu (742-9667) and **Kayak Kauai-Na Pali Outfitters** in Hanalei (926-9844). A full-day excursion costs $125 per person including lunch.

KAUAI: WAIMEA CANYON

In 1993, Kauai's tourist industry was rebuilding after the
devastation of Hurricane Iniki. In many areas of the
island, trees and other foliage suffered heavy damage.
However, Kauai's natural wonders remain intact, including Waimea Canyon and Kokee State Park. Hiking trails
lace Kokee State Park, and a short drive reveals one of
the Hawaiian islands' most spectacular views from the
Kalalau Valley Lookout into Waimea Canyon and the
Alakai Jungle.

Suggested Schedule

7:00 a.m.	Set out for Waimea Canyon after an early breakfast in Kapaa.
9:00 a.m.	Kilohana.
11:00 a.m.	Hanapepe.
11:15 a.m.	Waimea.
11:45 a.m.	Waimea Canyon Road.
12:00 noon	Waimea Canyon Lookout.
12:30 p.m.	Puu Hinahina Lookout.
1:00 p.m.	Lunch at Kokee Lodge Restaurant.
1:45 p.m.	Kokee Natural History Museum.
2:15 p.m.	Drive to Kalalau Lookout.
3:00 p.m.	Drive to Makaha Ridge.
4:00 p.m.	Iliau Nature Loop Trail for sunset views.
5:00 p.m.	Return to Highway 50 on Kokee Road and east on Highway 50.
5:30 p.m.	Dinner in Hanapepe at the Green Garden.
7:00 p.m.	Check into your Poipu accommodations.
8:00 p.m.	Enjoy the nightlife along Poipu Beach.

Beaches of Kauai

CAUTION! Starting at Nukolii Beach, north of Lihue,
North Shore beaches can be extremely treacherous for
swimmers. Wailua Beach is beautiful, but heavy surf
causes a strong backwash. Kapaa Beach is all right at low
tide, thanks to reef protection, especially north of the

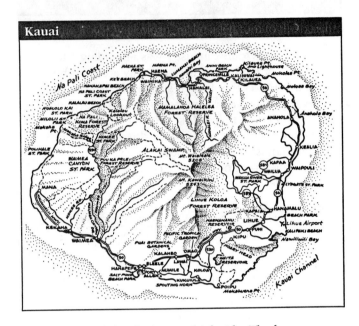

Waikaea Canal, but beware at high tide. The bays on
either side of Anapalau Point, reached by the old coast
road paralleling Kealia Beach, and Opana Beach north of
Opana Point, have some of the island's best snorkeling,
using appropriate caution. Rough waters, surface currents, and backwash make most of the North Shore
beaches dangerous. This is true at Kealia Beach,
Aliomanu Beach, Kukuna Beach, Moloaa Beach,
Kaakaaniu Beach, Waipake Beach, and others to Kilauea
Bay and Kilauea Point National Wildlife Refuge. Near
Princeville, there's no safe swimming until Hanalei Pier,
and even there swimming can be unsafe due to rip currents in winter. Stay close to shore. Kahalahala and
Lumahai beaches are as dangerous as they are beautiful.
They are for gazing at but not for swimming. The same is
true for Wainiha Beach, Wainiha Kuau Beach, Kaonihi
and Kanaha beaches, and Makua Beach, where you can
snorkel inside the reef. Both Haena Beach and Kee
Beach are not for swimming. In other words, *don't swim
outside protected areas on the North Shore.*

Sightseeing Highlights

▲▲▲Kilohana (245-7818)—Located nearby on Highway 50, Kilohana (superior or not to be surpassed) completely contrasts with Kukio Shopping Center and lives up to the meaning of its name. This elegant plantation home once was the most expensive house built on Kauai. Owner Gaylord Wilcox, nephew of the founder of Grove Farm Homestead, made it the center of uppercrust social, cultural and business life in the mid-1930s heyday of Hawaii's sugar industry. Open to the public as a house/museum and posh shopping place, Kilohana has been painstakingly restored with many of its original furnishings and artifacts.

▲Hanapepe—En route to Hanapepe, follow Highway 570 toward the McBryde Mill, about a mile east of Port Allen, and turn on the cane road toward the ocean to find Wahiawa Beach, one of Kauai's loveliest and most protected beaches. Back to the main road (unless you decide to stay at the beach), a mile past Eleele, a panoramic view opens from Hanapepe Lookout over lush and scenic Hanapepe Valley. The town is entered past Hanapepe Canyon Lookout at the lush mouth of a green valley planted in taro between red cliffs. The town's wooden buildings hang over the west bank of the river. Besides the canyon view, the best attractions in town are the Green Garden Restaurant and several excellent art galleries. This former near "ghost town" is renewing rapidly and will be one of the most interesting tiny towns on Kauai.

▲Waimea—This town is full of history: missionary and English, American, and Russian settlements and churches; the oldest house on the island (Gulick-Rowell House); star-shaped Fort Elizabeth (not much left to see, unfortunately); and, across the river, Captain Cook's 1778 landing site.

▲▲▲Waimea Canyon—The canyon is best seen in early morning light, so beat the tour buses to the three viewing platforms. The 3,000-foot gorge cuts a jagged swath of mossy greens and blues into the reddish brown volcanic walls of the Kokee Plateau. Easily accessible

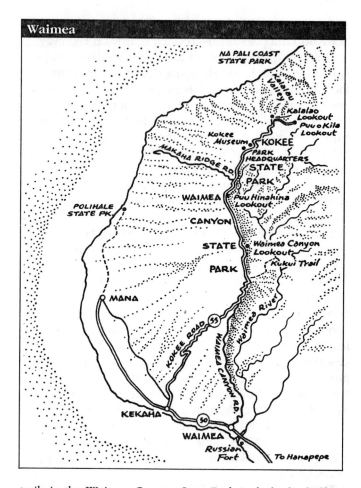

trails in the Waimea Canyon State Park include the half-mile round-trip Iliau Nature Loop (halfway between the 8- and 9-mile markers), offering excellent views of the canyon and Waialae Falls on the other side, and the strenuous 3-mile Kukui Trail switchbacking down the west canyon wall to the river below. Your best views, however, will be above Kokee Camps at Puu Ka Pele Lookout at the top of the gorge. Watch the jagged shapes of the gorge change color with the sun. Pick up a Kokee Trails map at the ranger station or the Kokee Natural History Museum, where you can book for the Kokee

Lodge and have lunch. Kauai Mountain Tours, P.O. Box
3069, Lihue, Kauai, HI 96766 (245-7224), has four-wheel-
drive tours to Kokee State Park and around Waimea
Canyon. $80 for seven hours, $40 for a half day.

▲▲▲**Kokee State Park**—This park covers 4,345 acres at
3,600 feet with 45 miles of hiking trails. The Kokee
Natural History Museum displays the park's flora and
fauna. It is open from 10:00 a.m. to 4:00 p.m. A lush
meadow set in a densely forested area is a good spot for
a picnic. The view is stunning from the lookout over
Kalalau Valley, with waterfalls and vegetation cascading
4,000 feet down the deepest valley on the Na Pali Coast.
Drive about a mile above the Kalalau Lookout to the Puu
O'Kila Lookout for another spectacular view of the Na
Pali Cliffs.

Where to Stay
Kokee Lodge's dozen cabins are furnished with everything you need for a stay of up to 5 days. Four newer 2-
bedroom cedar cabins sleeping up to six rent for $45.
Four duplex units containing large studios rent for $35;
two other 2-bedrooms and two small studios also rent for
$35. ($25 cabins are a thing of the past, but these still are
among the best deals in Hawaii.) Definitely reserve
ahead: P.O. Box 819, Waimea, HI 96796, 335-6061. Next
to Kahili Mountain Park (see Itinerary Options), a few
steps from a good snorkeling beach and the Beach
House Restaurant, Den and Dee Wilson's **Prince Kuhio
Condominiums**, 5160 Lawai Rd., Koloa, Kauai, (742-
1409 or toll-free 800-722-1409) are one of the best hotel
or condo deals in Poipu. Their $69 (to $79) double
rooms become a $296 weekly rate for a very nicely fur-
nished apartment overlooking Prince Kuhio Park or gardens on the grounds. Prices are higher December 15 to
April 15, as is true everywhere on Kauai except at the
Kauai YMCA's **Camp Naue** in Haena and the YWCA's
Camp Sloggett in Kokee with beautiful hiking trails all
around. Purchase a $10 membership card and for $12 per
night you get a mattress, space in the dormitory, and
kitchen and shower facilities. Write: YMCA, 3094 Elua,

Lihue, HI 96766, 245-5959; YWCA, P.O. Box 1786, Lihue, HI 96766, 246-9090.

Near Spouting Horn, facing the surf and rocky coastline, **Gloria's Spouting Horn Bed & Breakfast**, 4464 Lawai Beach Road, Koloa, Kauai, HI 96756, 742-6995, offers charming accommodations, mostly with ocean views, tasty and ample breakfasts, and very reasonable rates for Poipu at $50 to $120. Eve Warner and Al Davis, who operate **Hawaii Bed & Breakfast Service**, P.O. Box 449, Kapaa, HI 96746 (822-7771 or toll-free 800-733-1632 or 800-822-2723) have built their own rental units behind their house near Poipu Beach Park. **Poipu Plantation**, 1792 Pe'e Rd., Koloa, has four 1-bedroom self-contained units, $70 to $80 for a garden view, $75 for an ocean view, and $85 for 2-bedroom units, ocean view, without breakfast. With a lovely garden, great location, and perfect hosts, you can't go wrong. Write Poipu Plantation, Route 1, Box 119, Koloa, HI 96756, 742-7038 or 822-7771.

The **Garden Isle Cottages**, 2666 Puuholu Road to your left as you head for Spouting Horn, offers a few of the least expensive local accommodations. Artists Sharon and Robert Flynn have a very comfortable and nicely decorated group of cottages in a garden setting and others scattered around the nearby area, $51 to $83 for a studio and $83 to $115 for a double for two persons. Write Garden Isle Cottages, R.R. 1, Box 355, Koloa, HI 96756, 742-6717. A very special treat at a moderate price is Hans and Sylvia Zeevat's **Koloa Landing Cottages**, 27 04B Hooonani Rd., with nicely designed, furnished, equipped, and cared for 2-bedroom cottages (only 2) at $75 single or double and studios at $50 single or double. Write Dolphin Realty, R.R. 1, Box 70, 2827 Poipu Road, Koloa, Kauai, HI 96756, 742-1470.

The Koloa area has some of the more unusual bed and breakfast and alternative accommodations on Kauai, away from the bustle of tourist activities but close to Koloa and Poipu Beach. Rustic **Kahili Mountain Park**, P.O. Box 298, Koloa, Kauai, HI 96756, 742-9921, operated by the Seventh Day Adventist Church, is located seven miles from Poipu Beach. Cabinettes with hot plates rent for $20 double, and cabins with a two-burner stove and sink rent for $35.

Where to Eat

In Hanapepe, the **Green Garden**, 335-5422, is a top restaurant choice for good and plentiful Hawaiian, Oriental, and American dishes such as barbecued chicken, tempura aki, breaded mahimahi, and incomparable home-baked pies. Plants are everywhere, the screened wall faces a garden, and you'll feel right at home. Get there before 8:30 p.m. (closed on Tuesdays). On the right-hand side of the street, before you come to the Green Garden, is a huge dining room that looks like a local fraternal club's banquet hall. At the **Koloa Broiler**, 742-9122, on Koloa Road, you order beef or mahimahi, cook it yourself on a central broiler, toast some fresh baked bread, and help yourself to the salad bar. For breakfast or lunch, definitely stop at the **Garden Isle Bake Shoppe** (6:30 a.m.-9:00 p.m.) in Kiahuna Shopping Village on Poipu Road, 742-6070. The **Beach House**, 742-7575, rebuilt after Hurricane Iwa and again after Iniki, has a beautiful setting on Spouting Horn Road but is the place to skip dinner and just have a Malihini Pupu Platter and drinks. The **Plantation Gardens Restaurant**, 742-1695, at the Kiahuna Plantation Resort, is one of the prettiest restaurants in the area, though you'll pay $20 to $30 per person for dinner, atmosphere, decor, crystal and silver, and the right wine.

The **Kokee Lodge restaurant** (335-6061) adjoining the gift shop, offers simple, basic, tasty snacks and dinners at moderate prices. After a few hours of walking or hiking, the food tastes very good.

Itinerary Options

Ka'lmi Na'auao Hawai'i Nei—Back on Highway 50, past the Kukuiolono Golf Course, which has a delightful Japanese garden and outstanding coastal views, 'Olu Pua Gardens spreads over 12 acres a half-mile past Kalaheo (on the mauka side). An estate originally built in the 1930s for the Alexander family, founders of Kauai's largest pineapple plantation, the decor, antiques, and furnishings of the house and its magnificent gardens and tree groves have been delighting visitors for years.

Now 'Olu Pua Gardens is shaping an exciting new direction as the Hawaiian cultural center for Kauai Ka 'Imi Na'auao Hawai'i Nei, the school of hula and Hawaiian culture. Special tours of the grounds combine Hawaiian lore and botanical information. Don't miss the **Saturday Heritage Garden Tour** (10:00 a.m. and 1:00 p.m., $15 per person).

Na Pali Coast: This area can be seen by foot, boat, or helicopter. By foot, hike the 11-mile Kalalau Trail. **Captain Zodiac Raft Expeditions**, 800-422-7824, offers a $95 full-day trip or a $75 morning or afternoon excursion; and **Blue Odyssey Adventures**, 826-9033, has morning, afternoon, and full-day excursions from Hanalei for $75 to $125. Zodiac boats are very tough motorized rubber rafts that are unsinkably safe. **Lady Ann Charters**, 245-8538, and **Whitey's Na Pali Cruises**, 926-9221, offer cruiser trips with snorkeling along the Na Pali Coast; also from Hanalei Bay.

Na Pali Zodiac helicopter trips, 826-9371 or 800-422-7824, are a thrilling (though expensive) way to see the Waimea Canyon and Na Pali Coast, especially early morning and sunset flights. The cost ranges from $100 to $200. Other reliable helicopter operations include **Papillon Helicopters**, 826-6591; **Jack Harter Helicopters**, 245-3774; or **Will Squire's Helicopter**, 245-7541.

KAUAI: POIPU

Poipu beaches, including hidden ones such as secluded Mahaulepu Beach, are as good as you'll find in Hawaii. Thousands of different kinds of flowers and plants can be seen in the Kiahuna Plantation Resort and Gardens in Poipu. Garden lovers also should make reservations for a tour of neighboring National Tropical Botanical Garden in Lawai Valley, a beautiful 186-acre garden estate. Browse through boutiques and galleries in Koloa's attractively refurbished nineteenth-century wooden buildings.

Suggested Schedule

8:00 a.m.	Breakfast in Koloa Town and pack a beach picnic at the Big Save Market.
9:00 a.m.	A morning at Poipu Beach or Shipwreck and Mahaulepu beaches.
12:00 noon	Picnic lunch at the beach.
1:30 p.m.	Return to Poipu, clean up, and head for Spouting Horn.
2:30 p.m.	Visit Kiahuna Gardens and Kiahuna Shopping Village.
4:00 p.m.	Back to Koloa Town for sightseeing and browsing.
5:00 p.m.	Sunset at the beach, Koloa Landing, or happy hour somewhere comfortable.
6:00 p.m.	Dinner and overnight in Poipu.

Sightseeing Highlights

Koloa—A plantation town that developed in the mid-1800s around a sugar mill, Koloa declined with the demise of the sugar industry until tourism in the early 1970s started the restoration of "Old Koloa Town." Along Highway 50 heading for the turnoff to Koloa, the beautiful route from Lihue aims at Knudsen Gap between the Haupu Range and the Kahili Ridge. Kawaikini and Waialeale peaks usually vanish into thick clouds. Highway 52 or Maluhia (Serenity) Road turns toward Koloa through a mile-long Tree Tunnel,

Australian eucalyptus trees planted in 1911 by Walter McBride to form a dramatic gateway to his sugar plantation domain. Rusty tin roofs, sagging and bulging walls, dilapidated porches, weathered timber, and other remnants of economic decline still visible in the 1980s have been painted over and prettified into "Old Koloa Town." Ruins of Kauai's first sugar mill remain as a picturesque relic of days when owners paid workers in scrip redeemable at the mill's grocery store. Down Hapa Road, off Weliweli Road, in the churchyard of St. Raphael's Church, Kauai's oldest Roman Catholic church, are the burial plots of plantation workers and their families. About three miles north of Poipu, picturesque Koloa today is a thriving shopping village with over 40 stores and restaurants.

▲▲▲**Poipu**—Sun-drenched beaches line Poipu's old sugarcane coast, boasting excellent swimming, snorkeling, diving, and surfing. Hotels and condominiums cluster along Poipu's playground of the alii where Hawaiian fishermen still mend their nets and talk story at popular Poipu Beach Park. The mahimahi T-shirts clinging to so many playful bodies on nearby Brennecke's Beach come from a popular lunch and drinking spot with beachgoers, Brennecke's Beach Broiler. From the lush tropical parklike setting of the condominium Kiahuna Plantation, once part of Hawaii's oldest sugarcane plantation, locals beachcomb among shore rocks for edible opihi. Meanwhile, inside deluxe shorefront restaurants, local seafood is served without this delicious tent-shaped mollusk—ironically because opihi is too expensive (almost $200 a gallon). Mahaulepu, several miles farther down the main cane road beyond Shipwreck, still possesses its "hidden" status. Enjoy scenic views of the coastline and mountains from a beach lined with ironwoods and the pleasures of swimming in tranquil ocean waters during summer months.

▲**Spouting Horn**—In the opposite direction from Poipu Beach, a submerged lava tube regularly produces the Spouting Horn geyser. Old-timers say that this geyser does not spout or moan as vigorously as it used to, but it still remains a major attraction for loads of tourists. Jewelry stands near the geyser's viewpoint offer some of the best deals on the island for coral shell jewelry and Niihau shell leis.

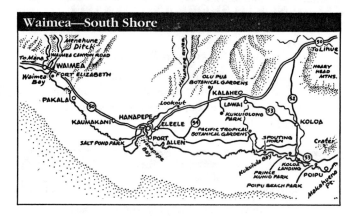

Waimea—South Shore

Itinerary Options

▲▲▲**National Tropical Botanical Garden**, located on Hailima Road about two miles south of Lawai, is the only tropical research garden in the United States. It has a staggering abundance of tropical flora in its collection, adding about a thousand plants each year. A 2-hour guided tour of the 186-acre site, only given on Tuesday and Thursday mornings at 9:00 a.m., costs $15 per person and requires advance reservations. (Write to Box 340, Lawai, Kauai, HI 96765; tel. 332-7361.) The tour includes the estate started by Queen Emma, wife of Kamehameha IV, in the 1870s and developed by the Allerton family.

Snorkeling and diving: Most resort hotels and condominiums have snorkeling gear free for guests. Otherwise rentals cost $5 to $15 a day. Dive shops located in Koloa, Wailua/Kapaa, and Hanalei offer one- and two-tank dives for $55 to $75 and certification courses for about $350. Up to 3 hours of scuba touring costs $55 including equipment, and a half-day dive costs about $75. Explore **Shell Graveyard**, an underwater cave at Hanalei Bay with **Sea Sage Diving Center**, 4-1378 Kuhio Highway, Kapaa, Hi 96746 (822-3841). **Captain Andy's Sailing Adventures** (822-7833) runs snorkel and sunset tours from Kukuiula Harbor in a trimaran.

KAUAI: NORTH SHORE AND HANALEI VALLEY

Hanalei is about 50 miles from Poipu. The ambitious goal of today's drive is to see and enjoy as many beach gems between Kapaa and Haena as possible and to take a leisurely drive along the scenic 9 miles between Hanalei and Haena Beach Park.

Suggested Schedule

7:00 a.m.	Early breakfast.
8:00 a.m.	Stop at Kealia, Anahola, and Moloaa beaches.
10:00 a.m.	Kong Lung Center, Lighthouse Road.
10:30 a.m.	Visit the Kilauea Lighthouse and Bird Sanctuary.
12:00 noon	Option: Picnic lunch at Secret Beach or Anini Beach.
2:00 p.m.	Hanalei Valley Lookout for a panoramic view of the river, the valley, and its taro fields against the background of the Na Pali Coast Range.
2:15 p.m.	Hanalei Town and Hanalei Beach.
2:45 p.m.	View of Lumahai Beach and Haena Beach Park en route to Kee Beach.
3:15 p.m.	Kee Beach.
4:30 p.m.	Return to Hanalei Town for sunset from the Hanalei pier over Hanalei Bay.
7:00 p.m.	Dinner in Hanalei and evening at the Tahiti Nui.

Orientation

North of Lihue, the Wailua River and Kapaa areas have a number of beautiful and fascinating historic and scenic places to visit that are saved for tomorrow: the Fern Grotto, ancient temples, beautiful waterfalls, gardens and a restored Hawaiian village, the Marketplace at Coconut Plantation, hiking trails, the Coco Palms resort, exploring and hiking around the Sleeping Giant in Kapaa and other attractions.

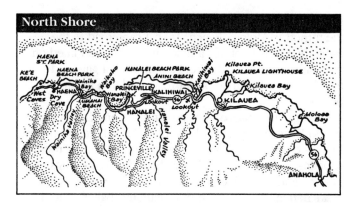

The lovely hidden beaches of the east coast extend to Secret Beach near the village of Kilauea, which has some special restaurants and shops, but the real attraction in the area is a fascinating coastal bird sanctuary. The Princeville Resort covers a huge area above Hanalei Valley and Hanalei, one of the most interesting villages of Hawaii. Shop, dine, visit some historical sites, join a luau, talk story, and relax or you'll miss the real Hanalei. A series of lovely beaches along the north shore leads to Haena Point, the end of the road and Kee Beach, beginning of the rugged Kalalau Valley Trail along the Na Pali Coast.

Sightseeing Highlights
▲▲Kealia Beach—This is the first in a string of beautiful white sand beaches north of Kapaa. From here take the scenic old coastal road almost to Anahola Bay where it returns to Highway 56.

▲▲Anahola Bay Beach Park—Just a few miles north of Kapaa, this beach is lovely for relaxation and picnics but hazardous for swimming.

▲▲Moloaa Beach—This beach is reached off the Koolau Road. Take a right turn off Highway 56 at the Papaya Plantation and Information Center. From Moloaa Bay take a right turn on Koolau Road to return to Highway 56.

▲▲Larson's Beach—A lovely narrow stretch of secluded sand, this beach is found (with difficulty) down the same Koolau Road, which you take for another mile past the turnoff to Moloaa Beach. Take a cane road to the right, then switch left for a mile onto a dirt road lined on both sides with barbed wire. Pass through a gate and travel another half-mile of dirt road until you reach the beach.

▲▲**Kong Lung Store**—Located in the Kong Lung Center in Old Kilauea Town, on the way to the lighthouse, this is Kauai's oldest plantation general store (1881). One room contains an art gallery with very high quality carvings, pottery, and other Pacific area items.

▲▲**Kilauea**—A collection of restaurants, bakeries, and shops off Lighthouse Road make Kilauea one of the most delightful places on Kauai for a refreshing break. Sylvester's Catholic Church is located just before the turn onto Kilauea Road to the lighthouse. It has an octagonal design made out of lava and native wood with interior murals of the stations of the cross painted by Jean Charlot, a well-known island artist.

▲▲**Secret Beach** (or Kauapea Beach)—One of the most beautiful, longest, and widest beaches in Hawaii. Turn left on Kauapea Road (.8 mile from Kong Lung). Watch on your right for a fence (with a marine reserve notice on it) and a dirt path down a long steep trail through beautiful tropical growth to the beach. Beautifully calm in summer, the waves get wicked in winter. As a secluded camping spot, and a favorite nude beach, it's hard to beat.

▲▲**The Kilauea Lighthouse and Bird Sanctuary**— Drive straight down Kilauea Road to the lighthouse with the largest "clamshell lens" in the world. It sends its beacon 90 miles out to sea. Permanent and migratory birds fill the peninsula, including the red-footed booby, the white-tailed and red-tailed tropic bird, the Laysan albatross, and the wedge-tailed shearwater. A small museum at the lighthouse has pictures of all the birds. The craggy point is under the protection of the U.S. Fish and Wildlife Service. You can borrow binoculars to look for green sea turtles, spinner dolphins, or whales in season. The Kilauea Point Refuge is open daily except Saturday from noon to 4:00 p.m. A $2 fee for each adult.

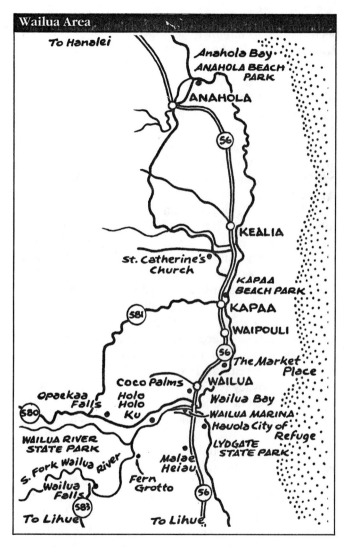

Wailua Area

To Hanalei

Anahola Bay
ANAHOLA BEACH PARK

ANAHOLA

56

KEALIA

St. Catherine's Church

KAPAA BEACH PARK

581

KAPAA

WAIPOULI

56

The Market Place

Coco Palms

Opaekaa Falls

Holo Holo Ku

580

WAILUA

Wailua Bay

WAILUA MARINA

Hauola City of Refuge

LYDGATE STATE PARK

WAILUA RIVER STATE PARK

S. Fork Wailua River

Malae Heiau

Wailua Falls

Fern Grotto

583

To Lihue

56

To Lihue

▲▲**Kalihiwai Beach**—Just past Kilauea down the Kalihiwai Road, you'll come to a dead end at a white sand beach lined by ironwoods which is perfect for sheltered camping. Swimming and bodysurfing are ideal in summer months. Swimming is safe in the lagoon where the river meets the ocean. The quiet little village on Kalihiwai Bay was destroyed by tidal waves in 1946 and 1957. You can walk along the beach from Secret Beach to Kalihiwai.

▲▲**Anini Beach**—Just before you reach Princeville on the second Kalihiwai Road, this beach is about a mile past the first one to the right just past the Kalihiwai Lookout and Princeville Airport. Turn on Anini Road to miles of white sand beach that is sheltered by the longest exposed reef off Kauai. This beach is great for windsurfing year-round and for summer swimming and snorkeling in the shallow water. Camping at the south end of the beach, with facilities, requires a county permit.

▲**Princeville**—On a royal vacation in 1860, Kamehameha IV, Queen Emma, and their son, Prince Albert, visited the rolling plateau overlooking Hanalei Bay. That regal event inspired its naming as Princeville. First a sugar plantation and then Kauai's largest cattle ranch, the 11,000-acre Princeville resort today is built around several championship golf courses, with thousands of acres of development still on the drawing boards. The new 252-room Sheraton Mirage Princeville, practically rebuilt after Hurricane Iniki on its old site, is one of the most elegant hotels in Hawaii in one of the most beautiful settings. For visitors who want more space and privacy for less money, the resort includes a variety of first-rate condominiums like the Hanalei Bay Resort, Puu Poa, 5380 Honoiki St., Hanalei, HI 96714 (800-827-4427 or 826-6522), with a secluded beach a short way down the hill; Pali Ke Kua, Ka Haku Rd., Princeville, Hanalei, Kauai, HI 96714 (826-9066 or toll-free 800-367-7042); and The Cliffs, P.O. Box 1005, Hanalei, HI 96714 (800-523-0411 or 826-6219). The 27-hole golf course has a greens fee of $40, plus $26 for a mandatory golf cart, for an exquisite round of golf.

▲**The Hanalei Valley Lookout**—Just past the entrance to Princeville, pull off to the left to view a patchwork of ancient taro fields that carpet the valley below. The Hanalei River is a silver loop as it flows placidly to Hanalei Bay, in turn cradled by a 3,500-foot protective pali. The village, river, and beautiful valley along its bank take their name from Hanalei (Crescent) Bay. The

Hanalei Lookout at the top of the hill before descending into Hanalei Valley frames one of the most spectacular and tranquil vistas in Hawaii, looking across terraced taro patches surrounding the Hanalei River as it weaves its way nine miles toward three magnificent mountains and a 3,500-foot pali over which more than a dozen waterfalls cascade.

Many taro growers in the valley cultivate their crops under the watchful eye of the U.S. Fish & Wildlife Service whose mission is to protect wildlife. Preserved as a National Wildlife Refuge, the valley is home to the Hawaiian duck, the stilt, and endangered Hawaiian gallinule. Over 900 acres of Hanalei Valley comprise the Hanalei National Wildlife Refuge. You can drive down Hanalei Valley Road but can't get out of your car except at the restored Haraguchi Rice Mill or at the end of the road.

▲**Hanalei**—Situated on Hanalei Bay below Princeville, Hanalei is reached by a narrow one-lane bridge crossing the Hanalei River that unintentionally serves as a blessed barrier to large, heavy tour buses and construction trucks. Cross the Hanalei River on Highway 56 over Hanalei Bridge, a steel bridge prefabricated in New York (of all places), erected in 1912, and now on the National Register of Historic Landmarks. For decades Hanalei has been the center of counterculture on Kauai and a gathering place for escapists of all types. Hanalei's hodgepodge of ramshackle and new buildings, including general stores, restaurants, museums, boutiques, galleries, and shops, appropriately reflects Hanalei's nonconformist charm and mystique. A notable departure from this unplanned pattern is the Old Hanalei School, on the National Register and recently refurbished for tourist-oriented shops and restaurants.

On the other end of town, behind Waioli Huiia Church, the Waioli Mission House Museum (245-3202) is the former residence of the Wilcoxes and other mid-eighteenth-century Protestant missionaries. Living rooms and bedrooms are full of interesting missionary artifacts and history. The museum is open Tuesdays, Thursdays, and Saturdays until 3:00 p.m.

▲▲**Haena Beach Park**—Just past Haena Point this beautiful white sand beach with coconut palms, lush foliage, and tall cliffs rises from the sea. With a camping permit, you can camp in this 5-acre park.

Haena Beach Park, across from Maniniholo Dry Cave, occasionally gets crowded. More secluded Haena beaches are located off access roads along Route 56.

▲▲**Kee Beach**—This is one of the most perfect beaches in Hawaii for picnicking, swimming, and snorkeling in summer and watching the high surf in winter months. Nearby are the remains of a heiau, the temple of the goddess of the hula where sacred dances were taught. Beyond are the cliffs of Na Pali and the beginning of the Kalalau Trail. The trailhead to Kalalau Valley is opposite the Kee parking area and clearly marked. Walk about a half-mile up the trail and look back for a wonderful view of Kee Beach and the Na Pali Coast.

Where to Stay

Susan and Don Akre (822-1075), hosts of the **Makana Inn**, have a 1-bedroom guest cottage with a king-size bed, overlooking Mt. Waialeale and lovely pastures, for $60 per night for a couple or a private 1-bedroom apartment downstairs with kitchenette at $50 per night per couple. A few miles from Kapaa Village, in a scenic fruit and vegetable growing valley called Kapahi reached by Kawaihau Road, the **Keapana Center** (822-7968) tucked in lush rolling hills offers peace, a jacuzzi overlooking beautiful mountain vistas, and panoramic views from the living room and private rooms, for $50 single and $60 double per night. Edee Seymour's **Victoria Place** (332-9300), a hillside B&B in Lawai, has three rooms and a studio apartment, beautiful gardens, healthful breakfasts, and aloha at $60 to $85.

Where to Eat

Norberto's El Cafe, 4-1373 Kuhio Highway, Kapaa, 822-3362, has opened an inexpensive and delicious restaurant in Hanalei. It doesn't look like much outside, but the food is great, including desserts that Mexican restaurants usually shun. **Duane's Ono-Char Burger** brings additional glory to the townlet of Anahola with delicious (*ono* in Hawaiian) burgers served from a busy roadside stand. Two choices of outstanding bakeries— **The Bread Also Rises** and **Jacques**—around the corner from one another in Kilauea, dispense unsurpassed choices of baked goods. The al fresco **Casa di Amici** (828-1388) serves delicious Italian food, pesto and alfredo sauces, and tasty pasta dishes like pasta with walnuts in a Romano cheese cream sauce. The **Shell House** at the intersection of Kuhio Highway and Aku Road (826-7977) serves three excellent meals a day.

Hanalei comes together day or night at the family-owned and friendly **Tahiti Nui** (826-6277) on Highway 56. Its weather-beaten exterior and thatched-wall interior are just right for a Hanalei beachcomber's watering hole. Nighttime entertainment mostly is spontaneous, mainly Hawaiian songs. Owner Auntie Louise Marston sometimes chimes in with her renditions of Tahitian songs and hula. The luau on Wednesday and Friday nights is deservedly popular, and reservations are essential. The Tahiti Nui's Tahitian owner has created the prime local gathering place, down-to-earth, casual and fun. Chef Jeff Bolman prepares consistently good lunches and dinners that are even better in the colorful, warm, relaxed, beach-shack atmosphere.

Itinerary Options
Westin Kauai and Lihue Area: Only two miles from the airport, the main sightseeing in Lihue is the Westin Kauai resort, which deserves a visit at least. Remember that this resort has one of the best beaches on the island (Kalapaki) and four restaurants that are among the best in Hawaii. Some visitors may be curious about the **Alekoko Fishpond**, a mullet-raising lagoon near Lihue supposedly built by the mysterious menehunes.

Kalalau Trail: The Kalalau trail, Haena State Park and the park's Kee Beach, begin at the end of Route 56. A short hike to **Kaulu o Laka Heiau**, sacred to Laka, goddess of the hula, reveals a most important hula shrine

where traditionally hula masters express devotion to
their hula mistress. Many legends surround this revered
heiau located behind the Allerton House. According to
the most famous legend, Pele transformed herself into a
mortal to join the hula festival and fell in love with Chief
Lohiau.

Day hikers can leave their cars (locked) at Kee Beach
and walk two miles to **Hanakapiai Valley**, a few ardu-
ous hours of hiking each way. As though by magic, a
white sand beach at Hanakapiai appears in summer and
disappears again in winter. For hikes beyond
Hanakapiai, permits are required and appropriate camping gear is necessary. Walking the trail to Kalalau nonstop takes a long, 9-hour day. This strenuous hike
requires good boots, backpack, waterproof tent, a small
stove, and light blanket or sleeping bag. Be prepared to
boil or chemically treat all water. The trail should be
hiked in two parts, with a break at Hanokoa on the way
in and Hanakapiai on the way out, and another
overnight at Kalalau Beach. (Don't try to return from
Hanakapiai in the dark!) Erosion caused by rain can
make the 11-mile trail hazardous between October and
May and also during June rains. From May to September,
the water is calm enough to land on Kalalau Beach in a
canoe. On a lovely trail through narrow, sheltered, once
thickly settled Hanakapiai Valley, continue to
Hanalapiai Falls, an easy hike (2 miles) for about an
hour. (You pass the turnoff to the falls on the main trail
down to the beach.)

Notice the abandoned taro patches, stone walls, and
house foundations, and a large stone chimney that is all
that remains of a small coffee mill. Guava and mango
trees bear succulent fruit here. Occupied a thousand
years ago by *kuaaina* (backcountry folk), villages surrounded by sacred temples and elaborate terraced farms
existed peacefully between high cliffs surrounding each
valley along the Na Pali Coast. Taro farmers and their
families worked Kalalau Valley until the 1920s. It is one
of the last untamed parts of the Hawaiian islands.

Rainy **Hanakoa** is four miles and two small valleys

away from Hanakapiai. At a leisurely pace, the hike should take less than three hours. Frequent switchbacks pass breathtaking drop-offs. If it's not raining in Hanakoa, many pools in the stream offer delightful places to swim. There are ample camping sites sheltered on old agricultural terraces. Remember that constant rain may cause slides on parts of the trail to **Hanakoa Falls**. Clear pools for swimming at these falls are delightful rewards for weary hikers.

From mid-May to early October, take a boat trip in relatively calm seas to see the wonders of the Na Pali Coast. Most tours are on heavy-duty 23-foot inflatable rafts made famous by Jacques Cousteau and started on Kauai by **Captain Zodiac**. Unlike other companies making trips to remote Nualolo and Milolii valleys, **Lady Ann Cruises** sails on a 38-foot boat out of Lihue. Guests can snorkel ashore, tour ruins of an ancient Hawaiian village, and have lunch on a Na Pali Coast beach. This unforgettable tour lasts 5½ to 6 hours. Shorter tours, including whale-watching in season (December 15-March 15), are provided year-round.

For an unusual experience, try a double-hulled canoe sail on Hanalei Bay with **Ancient Hawaiian Adventures**, 826-6088.

In the Hanalei area, **Pooku Stables**, 826-6777, offers horse treks on the beach, to nearby waterfalls, and into the hills overlooking Hanalei Valley for wonderful views.

Charter Fishing: From May to August yellowfin tuna are running. Year-round you might catch marlin, mahimahi, ono, and bonita. Charters run $85 per person for a half day, $145 for a full day. Sea Breeze Sport Fishing Charters (828-1285) departs from Anini and Port Allen. Sport Fishing Kauai (742-7013) operates out of Kukuiula. Harbor and Coastal Charters (82-7007) out of Nawiliwali.

Helicopter tours: There is no better way to see Kauai, its Na Pali cliffs, Waialeale Mountain, and the island's wilderness interior than by helicopter. Helicopter companies charge about $130 for a 50-minute whirlibird ride. Jack Harter Helicopters (245-3774), has a helipad at

the Westin Kauai; Papillon Helicopters (826-6591) at
Princeville Airport offers two tours that land in the
wilderness for a swim and picnic lunch ($150) or a
champagne lunch ($250); Niihau Helicopters (335-3500)
offers two tours ($185 and $235) departing from the
Port Allen Airport for Niihau. Others are Ohana
Helicopters (245-3774), Will Squyres Helicopter Service
(245-7541), and South Seas Helicopters (245-7781).

KAUAI: WAILUA RIVER STATE PARK AND LIHUE

The final day in Hawaii presents choices for different tastes. If you can tolerate quantities of tourists, Wailua River State Park, the former home of Hawaii's royalty midway along the east coast, is well worth the visit. Otherwise, between Lihue and Wailua, you can swim, snorkel, whale watch, hike, or engage in any other favorite activities. Kauai has direct flights to the West Coast, but excursion airfares may require that you return to the U.S. mainland through Honolulu. An interisland flight in the late afternoon can be arranged to conveniently connect with a flight to the mainland.

Suggested Schedule	
8:00 a.m.	Breakfast and checkout.
9:00 a.m.	Wailua River State Park or other activity.
12:00 noon	Leisurely lunch and last minute shopping.
3:00 p.m.	Return rental car at the airport.
4:00 p.m.	Interisland flight to Honolulu.
6:00 p.m.	Return flight to the mainland.

Sightseeing Highlights
Wailua River Area—A really pretty beach lies hidden behind the Wailua Golf Course reached by a dirt road along the southern end of the links off Highway 56. Lengthy Wailua Beach provides many enjoyable places for swimming, picnicking, and unofficial camping. The remains of an ancient place of refuge and one of many heiaus along the river are found in Lydgate State Park at Leho Drive, just south of the Wailua River. Along a rugged stretch of coast fringed by magnificent ironwoods, you can swim safely (even children) and snorkel in clear water fronting Lydgate Park's white sand beach.

One of the most popular—and beautiful—tourist attractions in Hawaii, the Fern Grotto, a huge rock amphitheater draped by ferns under a cascade of water, is 3 miles up Wailua River, reachable only by a 20-minute boat ride ($10 for adults, half price for children). Contact Smith's Motor Boat Service (822-4111) and Waialeale Boat Tours (822-4908) for a 2-mile ride up the Wailua River.

Smith's Tropical Paradise, a 30-acre botanical garden, is filled with a marked collection of Kauai's ordinary, rare, and exotic foliage. Plywood facsimiles of Japanese, Philippine, and Polynesian villages can be bypassed, but the botanical garden is worth seeing. A guided tram tour costs $7. Open 8:30 a.m. to 4:30 p.m., regular admission for adults is $3 and $1.50 for children. (The luau/musical show in the evening—$12 for the show and $45 for the food—is as good as any that you'll see on the island with the exception of the incomparably spirited and unpretentious luau at the Tahiti Nui in Hanalei.)

From Highway 56 at Coco Palms, take a left on Route 580 toward Opaekaa Falls. Several miles up Route 580, Wailua State Park protects the river, and across the road is lovely Opaekaa Falls and Lookout. Across the road at the Lookout, a Hawaiian family has put together Kamokila Hawaiian Village. The road down on the left just before getting to the falls leads to the village on an island above the Wailua River. Restored thatched homes, a sleeping house, an eating house with utensils, herbalist's house, taro patches, ancient implements, demonstrations of poi-pounding and preparation of medicinal plants all are part of the guided tour. Hula dancing and other Hawaiian entertainment are scheduled at regular intervals.

▲**Kapaa and Waipouli**—Coco Palms Resort, situated amid 45 acres of coconut trees and including a lagoon, is renowned for its nightly torchlight ceremony. On the *makai* side of Route 56, the Sheraton Coconut Beach with lovely grounds and a popular nightly luau is the northern anchor of Coconut Plantation Resort. Kapaa Village stretched along Route 56 begins just north of the Plantation. Coconut Plantation includes other hotels, condos, and the Market Place at Coconut Plantation.

The more than 70 shops in the Market Place include some of the more interesting shopping for art and crafts on Kauai.

Where to Eat

Gaylord's, 245-9593, at Kilohana, might stretch the dwindling remainder of your budget for dinner, but for lunch it is reasonable. The setting (see Itinerary Options, below) and the food are special. As the last meal before heading to the mainland, and to celebrate your 22-day journey, I can't think of a better place. Fish of the day, chicken, duck, or vegetarian dishes, pasta, or Gaylord's Papaya Runneth Over (stuffed with baby shrimp), with Chocolate Decadence Cake or other delicious desserts, make for a fitting feast. The **Hanamaulu Restaurant and Tea House**, 245-2511, 4 miles north on Highway 56, also serves a perfect farewell meal. The beautifully landscaped garden, complete with stone pagoda and a carp pond, is the setting for Chinese and Japanese plate lunches that compare with the best on the islands.

Itinerary Options

In Nawiliwili, about halfway up Nawiliwili Road (Highway 58), the **Grove Farm Homestead** was founded as a sugarcane plantation in 1864 by the son of a Hanalei missionary family. Today the main house, plantation office, workers' cottages and outbuildings, orchards, and gardens are well preserved for tourists. Seeing the homestead requires more preplanning than most other attractions. Tours are provided only on Monday, Wednesday, and Thursday at 10:00 a.m. and 1:15 p.m. and last about 2 hours. The cost is about $3. Write to Grove Farm Homestead, P.O. Box 1631, Lihue, Kauai, HI 96766, or call 245-3202 at least a month in advance.

Kauai Museum, 245-6931, on Rice Street, has a permanent natural history collection and changing Hawaiiana exhibits. The book and gift shop is a good place to pick up souvenirs of your trip. The museum is open Monday through Friday, from 9:30 a.m. to 4:00 p.m., and admission is $3 for adults, children free.

If you have extra time, from Highway 56 take Highway 580 for 6.6 miles to the trailhead of **Kuilai Ridge Trail**, a 2-hour hike past waterfalls and orchids to two spectacular coast view points.

Lady Anne Cruises, 245-8538, has a 2-hour whale-watching cruise for $35, leaving Lihue at 9:00 a.m. with an expert commentator from the Pacific Whale Foundation.

Hiking: Three miles up the Wailua River, **Keahua Arboretum** is an ideal place to picnic and swim. Take Route 580 to the University of Hawaii Agricultural Experiment Station, and drive about 2 miles to the Keahua Stream where the trailhead starts just past the stream. The **Keahua Trail** is about a half-mile long through a forest reserve maintained by the Division of Forestry where marked posts identify many varieties of native and exotic plants and trees. From the Keahua Trail, a panorama of the coastline opens to the east and the Makaleha ("eyes looking about as in wonder") Mountains to the northwest. The trail through the Arboretum is a half-mile long.

Farther north, Sleeping Giant mountain behind Coco Palms shelters an undulating valley and beautiful forest reserve trails on the perimeter reached by Route 581 or 58 to the end of Waipouli Road. **Nonou Mountain Trail** (east side) begins off Haleilio Road, 1.2 miles from the junction of Routes 56 and 580, in the Wailua House lots behind the Sleeping Giant and climbs 1,250 feet to its summit. The **west side trail** starts on Route 581 and joins the **east side trail** at a picnic area about 250 feet below the summit in the **Nonou Forest Reserve.**

INDEX

Other Books from John Muir Publications

Asia Through the Back Door, 4th ed., 400 pp. $16.95 (available 7/93)
Belize: A Natural Destination, 336 pp. $16.95
Costa Rica: A Natural Destination, 2nd ed., 310 pp. $16.95
Elderhostels: The Students' Choice, 2nd ed., 304 pp. $15.95
Environmental Vacations: Volunteer Projects to Save the Planet, 2nd ed., 248 pp. $16.95
Europe 101: History & Art for the Traveler, 4th ed., 350 pp. $15.95
Europe Through the Back Door, 11th ed., 432 pp. $17.95
Europe Through the Back Door Phrase Book: French, 160 pp. $4.95
Europe Through the Back Door Phrase Book: German, 160 pp. $4.95
Europe Through the Back Door Phrase Book: Italian, 168 pp. $4.95
Europe Through the Back Door Phrase Book: Spanish & Portuguese, 288 pp. $4.95
A Foreign Visitor's Guide to America, 224 pp. $12.95
Great Cities of Eastern Europe, 256 pp. $16.95
Guatemala: A Natural Destination, 336 pp. $16.95
Indian America: A Traveler's Companion, 4th ed., 448 pp. $17.95 (available 7/93)
Interior Furnishings Southwest, 256 pp. $19.95
Mona Winks: Self-Guided Tours of Europe's Top Museums, 2nd ed., 448 pp. $16.95
Opera! The Guide to Western Europe's Great Houses, 296 pp. $18.95
Paintbrushes and Pistols: How the Taos Artists Sold the West, 288 pp. $17.95
The People's Guide to Mexico, 9th ed., 608 pp. $18.95
Ranch Vacations: The Complete Guide to Guest and Resort, Fly-Fishing, and Cross-Country Skiing Ranches, 2nd ed., 396 pp. $18.95
The Shopper's Guide to Art and Crafts in the Hawaiian Islands, 272 pp. $13.95
The Shopper's Guide to Mexico, 224 pp. $9.95
Understanding Europeans, 272 pp. $14.95
Undiscovered Islands of the Caribbean, 3rd ed., 288 pp. $14.95
Undiscovered Islands of the Mediterranean, 2nd ed., 224 pp. $13.95
Undiscovered Islands of the U.S. and Canadian West Coast, 288 pp. $12.95
Unique Colorado, 112 pp. $10.95 (available 6/93)
Unique Florida, 112 pp. $10.95 (available 7/93)
Unique New Mexico, 112 pp. $10.95 (available 6/93)
A Viewer's Guide to Art: A Glossary of Gods, People, and Creatures, 144 pp. $10.95
The Visitor's Guide to the Birds of the Eastern National Parks: United States and Canada, 410 pp. $15.95

2 to 22 Days Series
Each title offers 22 flexible daily itineraries useful for planning vacations of any length. Aside from valuable general information, included are "must see" attractions *and* hidden "jewels."
2 to 22 Days in the American Southwest, 1993 ed., 176 pp. $10.95
2 to 22 Days in Asia, 1993 ed., 176 pp. $9.95
2 to 22 Days in Australia, 1993 ed., 192 pp. $9.95

2 to 22 Days in California, 1993 ed., 192 pp. $9.95
2 to 22 Days in Europe, 1993 ed., 288 pp. $13.95
2 to 22 Days in Florida, 1993 ed., 192 pp. $10.95
2 to 22 Days in France, 1993 ed., 192 pp. $10.95
2 to 22 Days in Germany, Austria, & Switzerland, 1993 ed., 224 pp. $10.95
2 to 22 Days in Great Britain, 1993 ed., 192 pp. $10.95
2 to 22 Days Around the Great Lakes, 1993 ed., 192 pp. $10.95
2 to 22 Days in Hawaii, 1993 ed., 192 pp. $9.95
2 to 22 Days in Italy, 208 pp. $10.95
2 to 22 Days in New England, 1993 ed., 192 pp. $10.95
2 to 22 Days in New Zealand, 1993 ed., 192 pp. $9.95
2 to 22 Days in Norway, Sweden, & Denmark, 1993 ed., 192 pp. $10.95
2 to 22 Days in the Pacific Northwest, 1993 ed., 192 pp. $10.95
2 to 22 Days in the Rockies, 1993 ed., 192 pp. $10.95
2 to 22 Days in Spain & Portugal, 192 pp. $10.95
2 to 22 Days in Texas, 1993 ed., 192 pp. $9.95
2 to 22 Days in Thailand, 1993 ed., 180 pp. $9.95
22 Days (or More) Around the World, 1993 ed., 264 pp. $12.95

Automotive Titles
How to Keep Your VW Alive, 15th ed., 464 pp. $21.95
How to Keep Your Subaru Alive 480 pp. $21.95
How to Keep Your Toyota Pickup Alive 392 pp. $21.95
How to Keep Your Datsun/Nissan Alive 544 pp. $21.95
The Greaseless Guide to Car Care Confidence, 224 pp. $14.95
Off-Road Emergency Repair & Survival, 160 pp. $9.95

TITLES FOR YOUNG READERS AGES 8 AND UP
"Kidding Around" Travel Guides for Young Readers
All the "Kidding Around" Travel guides are 64 pages and $9.95 paper,
except for **Kidding Around Spain** and **Kidding Around the National
Parks of the Southwest,** which are 108 pages and $12.95 paper.
Kidding Around Atlanta
Kidding Around Boston,2nd ed.
Kidding Around Chicago, 2nd ed.
Kidding Around the Hawaiian Islands
Kidding Around London
Kidding Around Los Angeles
Kidding Around the National Parks of the Southwest
Kidding Around New York City, 2nd ed.
Kidding Around Paris
Kidding Around Philadelphia
Kidding Around San Diego
Kidding Around San Francisco
Kidding Around Santa Fe
Kidding Around Seattle
Kidding Around Spain
Kidding Around Washington, D.C., 2nd ed.

"Extremely Weird" Series for Young Readers. Written by Sarah
Lovett, each is 48 pages and $9.95 paper.
Extremely Weird Bats
Extremely Weird Birds
Extremely Weird Endangered Species
Extremely Weird Fishes
Extremely Weird Frogs

Extremely Weird Insects
Extremely Weird Mammals (available 8/93)
Extremely Weird Micro Monsters (available 8/93)
Extremely Weird Primates
Extremely Weird Reptiles
Extremely Weird Sea Creatures
Extremely Weird Snakes (available 8/93)
Extremely Weird Spiders

"Masters of Motion" Series for Young Readers. Each title is 48 pages and $9.95 paper.
How to Drive an Indy Race Car
How to Fly a 747
How to Fly the Space Shuttle

"X-ray Vision" Series for Young Readers. Each title is 48 pages and $9.95 paper.
Looking Inside Cartoon Animation
Looking Inside Sports Aerodynamics
Looking Inside the Brain
Looking Inside Sunken Treasure
Looking Inside Telescopes and the Night Sky

Multicultural Titles for Young Readers
Native Artists of North America, 48 pp. $14.95 hardcover
The Indian Way: Learning to Communicate with Mother Earth, 114 pp. $9.95
The Kids' Environment Book: What's Awry and Why, 192 pp. $13.95
Kids Explore America's African-American Heritage, 112 pp. $8.95
Kids Explore America's Hispanic Heritage, 112 pp. $7.95

Environmental Titles for Young Readers
Rads, Ergs, and Cheeseburgers: The Kids' Guide to Energy and the Environment, 108 pp. $12.95
Habitats: Where the Wild Things Live, 48 pp. $9.95
The Kids' Environment Book: What's Awry and Why, 192 pp. $13.95

Ordering Information
Please check your local bookstore for our books, or call 1-800-888-7504 to order direct from us. All orders are shipped via UPS; see chart below to calculate your shipping charge to U.S. destinations. **No P.O. Boxes please; we must have a street address to ensure delivery.** If the book you request is not available, we will hold your check until we can ship it. Foreign orders will be shipped surface rate unless otherwise requested; please enclose $3.00 for the first item and $1.00 for each additional item.

For U.S. Orders Totaling	Add	For U.S. Orders Totaling	Add
Up to $15.00	$4.25	$45.01 to $75.00	$6.25
$15.01 to $45.00	$5.25	$75.01 or more	$7.25

Methods of Payment
Check, money order, American Express, MasterCard, or Visa. We cannot be responsible for cash sent through the mail. For credit card orders, include your card number, expiration date, and your signature, or call (800) 888-7504. American Express card orders can be shipped only to billing address of cardholder. Sorry, no C.O.D.'s. Residents of sunny New Mexico, add 6.125% tax to total.

Address all orders and inquiries to:
John Muir Publications
P.O. Box 613
Santa Fe, NM 87504
(505) 982-4078
(800) 888-7504